P9-CSG-959

THE
BEST
AMERICAN
POETRY
2012

◊   ◊   ◊

Mark Doty, Editor

David Lehman, Series Editor

SCRIBNER POETRY
NEW YORK   LONDON   TORONTO   SYDNEY   NEW DELHI

BOCA RATON PUBLIC LIBRARY
BOCA RATON, FLORIDA

SCRIBNER POETRY

A Division of Simon & Schuster, Inc.
1230 Avenue of the Americas
New York, NY 10020

This book is a work of fiction. Names, characters, places, and incidents
either are products of the author's imagination or are used fictitiously. Any resemblance to
actual events or locales or persons, living or dead, is entirely coincidental.

Copyright © 2012 by David Lehman
Foreword copyright © 2012 by David Lehman
Introduction copyright © 2012 by Mark Doty

All rights reserved, including the right to reproduce this book or portions thereof
in any form whatsoever. For information address Scribner Subsidiary Rights
Department, 1230 Avenue of the Americas, New York, NY 10020.

First Scribner edition September 2012

SCRIBNER POETRY and design are registered trademarks of The Gale Group,
Inc., used under license by Simon & Schuster, Inc., the publisher of this work.

For information about special discounts for bulk purchases,
please contact Simon & Schuster Special Sales at 1-866-506-1949
or business@simonandschuster.com.

The Simon & Schuster Speakers Bureau can bring authors to your live event.
For more information or to book an event contact the Simon & Schuster Speakers
Bureau at 1-866-248-3049 or visit our website at www.simonspeakers.com.

Manufactured in the United States of America

1   3   5   7   9   10   8   6   4   2

Library of Congress Control Number: 88644281

ISBN 978-1-4391-8153-9
ISBN 978-1-4391-8152-2 (pbk)
ISBN 978-1-4391-8154-6 (ebook)

BOCA RATON PUBLIC LIBRARY
BOCA RATON, FLORIDA

CONTENTS

David Lehman was born in New York City in 1948. He was educated at Columbia University, spent two years in England as a Kellett Fellow at Cambridge University, and worked as Lionel Trilling's research assistant upon his return to New York. Lehman initiated *The Best American Poetry* series in 1988. He has received a Guggenheim Fellowship and an award in literature from the American Academy of Arts and Letters. His books of poetry include *Yeshiva Boys* (2009), *When a Woman Loves a Man* (2005), *The Evening Sun* (2002), *The Daily Mirror* (2000), and *Valentine Place* (1996), all from Scribner, as well as *Operation Memory* (1990) and *An Alternative to Speech* (1986), from Princeton University Press. He has edited *The Oxford Book of American Poetry* (Oxford University Press, 2006). *A Fine Romance: Jewish Songwriters, American Songs* (Nextbook/ Schocken), the most recent of his six nonfiction books, won the Deems Taylor Award from the American Society of Composers, Authors, and Publishers (ASCAP) in 2010. Lehman wrote and designed an exhibit based on the book, which visited fifty-five libraries in twenty-seven states on a tour sponsored by the American Library Association. He teaches in the graduate writing program of the New School in New York City.

FOREWORD

by David Lehman

◊　◊　◊

A few years ago my wife and I moved into a New York apartment house with a flower shop on the ground level. As an inveterate anthologist who loves flowers and likes picking up a last-minute rose, I took it as an auspicious sign that the shop is called Anthology. It is a splendid name for a florist: "anthology" derives from the Greek words for "flower" and "collection." The horticultural meaning preceded the literary sense, and editors of poetry books gathered "flowers of verse" long before a French revolutionist published his "flowers of evil." It is good to have a daily reminder of this connection between poems and "glowing violets," "fair musk-rose blooms," and daffodils "with the green world they live in," for the making of an anthology is only incidentally like the art of flower arrangement. In practice it can be a pretty fraught affair. If it is successful, the endeavor will generate discussion and debate, some of it heated, even pugnacious, and more appropriate to a fight club than to a quiet bower, where "the mind, from pleasure less, / Withdraws into its happiness."

"If you want to start an argument, put together an anthology, especially one that claims to be comprehensive," a jazz reviewer notes. "No matter how noble the intent, it invites disaffection. Make the subject area jazz, and you create a minefield of sensitive historical, political, social and musical issues. It's a treacherous endeavor—as is reviewing it."[1] The statement remains true if you substitute "exclusive" for "comprehensive" and "poetry" for "jazz." On the other hand, it's a sure proof that you're doing your job if your anthology quickens argument and dispute. People like anthologies—there's something for everyone. Practitioners like being in them, spectators like knowing who's in and who's out, critics like laying down the law, and malcontents like the

---

1. Stuart Isacoff, "Anthology by Committee," *The Wall Street Journal,* April 28, 2011.

occasion to air their grievances. As for the maker of poetry anthologies in particular, there is the gratification of reaching an educated readership for the elusive but vital art form whose death has so often been predicted. Something beyond nobility, something in defiance of disaffection and even treachery, is at work here. Pascal's aphorism has a special application to poetry and its devotees: the heart has its reasons that reason can only guess at.

The Best American Poetry 2012 is the twenty-fifth volume in the series—twenty-sixth if you count Harold Bloom's 1998 distillation, *The Best of the Best American Poetry, 1988–1997*. The books have provided a template for similar annuals from other nations. On my desk as I write, I have the 2009 volume of *The Best Canadian Poetry in English* (ed. A. F. Moritz, series ed. Molly Peacock) and *The Best Australian Poems 2011* (ed. John Tranter), each with its compelling new voices. *The Best Irish Poetry 2010,* ed. Matthew Sweeney, joins the famous (Seamus Heaney) and the emerging (Leanne O'Sullivan) in the time-honored fashion. *The Best New Zealand Poems,* which got its start in 2001, explains on its home page that "We have shamelessly modeled this online project on the successful US paperback anthology, *The Best American Poetry.* Each year we publish twenty-five poems from recent literary magazines and poetry collections, where possible including notes about and by the poet, as well as links to related publishing and literary websites. In this way we hope that readers will be able to follow up fresh discoveries. There are plenty to be made." Last year brought a welcome newcomer, *The Best British Poetry 2011* (ed. Roddy Lumsden). Other than consisting of seventy rather than seventy-five poems, the venture employs the identical structure and even the same typeface and design as *The Best American Poetry.* If there is one assumption common to all these "best of" books, it is that poetry has managed to thrive in the face of all the technological changes that seem, on the surface at least, so hostile to the muse.

Reporters are interested in trends, and you, cornered, may feel the impulse to invent one out of whole cloth just to please an interviewer. But I feel confident in my prediction that more and more arranged marriages will be taking place between poetry and video—confident enough to call this development a trend. Tom Devaney's online *ONandOnScreen* is devoted to poets' pairing their work with a video of their choice. The aim is a dialogue between "moving words and moving images" in the expectation that the "essential strangeness" of each medium will be enhanced. In 2011, *The Best American Poetry* partnered with Motionpoems, a Minneapolis-based poetry and video initiative founded by Todd Boss, himself a poet whose work has appeared in this series, and the animator Angella Kassube. Motionpoems commissioned video artists—commercial and freelance animators, filmmakers, musicians, sound designers, and producers—to make short films of poems chosen from *The Best American Poetry 2011*.[2] Where the poets choose their visual accompaniment in Devaney's project, Motionpoems reverses the order. The animators pick the poems and take it from there. To this observer, the dozen Motionpoems screened in October 2011 vindicated the concept of such "passive collaborations" between poets and visual artists, passive only in the sense that the poet's job is done after writing the poem and the video-maker is on his or her own. The idea of basing a video on a poem may one day seem as natural and inevitable as the setting of poems to music used to be.

While I am not sure that it constitutes a trend, exactly, I believe that the "uncanny" is a category too little invoked in discussions of American poetry. The poets of our time are drawn to ghostly demarcations, spectral presences. There are ghosts in the machine, ghosts in the martini, and they turn up regularly—angelic or demonic, benevolent or cruel—in poems. When, in late December, a senior editor at National Public Radio asked me to name three of my favorite poems of 2011 and to record some thoughts about them, I noticed only after assembling the trio that they share this quality of mystery and the uncanny, offering a spooky but also exhilarating glimpse of a spiritual world beyond our own. Mark Strand's "The Mysterious Arrival of an Unusual Letter," a prose poem, owes something of its effect to its brevity; it contains all of ten sentences, most of them short. The poet tells us about arriving home one night after a grueling day at the office. On the table he sees an envelope with his name on it. "The handwriting was my father's, but he had been dead for forty years. As one might, I began to think that maybe, just maybe, he was alive, living a secret life somewhere nearby. How else to explain the envelope? To steady myself, I sat down, opened it, and pulled out the letter. 'Dear Son,' was the way it began. 'Dear Son' and then nothing." The poem ends there, as eerie as a dream visitation from a deceased parent or lover.

2. Films based on poems by Erin Belieu, Matthew Dickman, K. A. Hays, Jane Hirshfield, L. S. Klatt, James Longenbach, Bridget Lowe, Eric Pankey, Mark Strand, David Wagoner, Richard Wilbur, and the series editor were shown in two public screenings at Open Book in Minneapolis on October 25, 2011.

Like Strand's poem, Stephanie Brown's "Notre Dame" was chosen by Mark Doty for *The Best American Poetry 2012*. Though not in prose, Brown's lines approach plain speech, an unadorned directness, eschewing the glamour of rhyme or traditional form. Brown describes staying with her family in an apartment near the great cathedral in Paris. One morning she wakes up and apprehends "two angels hovering" to protect her younger son. Only when the poem ends do we get the full context of this vision or waking dream: "It's sad to walk around the Seine when you are getting divorced while everyone else / Is kissing and filming their honeymoons or new loves. Even / My husband, after we got back together, laughed at that. / Because he, too, had been heartsick on another part of the planet."

My third pick was Paul Violi's "Now I'll Never Be Able to Finish That Poem to Bob" in the Brooklyn-based literary magazine *Hanging Loose.*[3] The poem is jolly and even madcap, featuring "a man in a chicken suit / handing out flyers on Houston Street" among other urban wonders. "It would have been a long poem," the poem concludes, "and it would have made a lot of sense / and shown why I believe Bob Hershon is a wise man." (Hershon edits *Hanging Loose*.) What makes the poem almost heartbreaking is the knowledge that Violi wrote it in the face of his own death. Diagnosed with pancreatic cancer in January 2011, this amazingly inventive poet died on April 2 and yet was able to infuse the writing of this, his last poem, with such high spirits that it almost becomes a cheerful missive to us from that other world from which no traveler has ever returned.

Our poems are haunted, as our lives are, by that unknown territory on the other side of a wall too high to climb and see over. In *The Best American Poetry 2012* the "spirit in the dark" comes to light in poems that consider "The Gods" and "The Afterlife," the stories of Magdalene and the road to Emmaus. The poems wonder where "we go after we die"; they whisper rumors of the other side, about which all we know for certain is that it is "something entirely else." Mark Doty, who chose the poems for this year's volume, has a keen ear for the poetry of the uncanny. In his poems he has explored heaven as an earthly possibility, has delved into the realm of dreams more real than waking life, has encountered the apparition of a deceased poet obliviously enjoying his lunch at "the Eros Diner, corner / of 21st Street." Doty has won acclaim for his poetry (*Fire to Fire: New and Selected Poems* won the National

---

3. The issue appeared in December, too late to be considered for this volume.

Book Award for Poetry in 2008) and his prose (*Dog Years* was a *New York Times* bestseller in 2007) not only in North America but in the United Kingdom, where he is the sole American ever to receive the T. S. Eliot Prize. He cares deeply about poetry and poets, loves the language, values good writing. He is as sympathetic a reader as I could have wanted, as generous, and as open to new voices. Mark writes about poetry with passion and acumen. Read him on Hart Crane or May Swenson, on William Blake's "Ah! Sunflower" and on Alan Shapiro's, in his book *The Art of Description,* and you will see why I felt he was an irresistible choice to edit this volume of *The Best American Poetry.*

To write poetry, to read it, to go to poetry readings, is a way of being in the world, and there will always be those who get suspicious and feel that maybe Plato was right to exclude the poets from his ideal Republic. Poetry, as they see it, is a form of "divine madness" that can lead you astray like a drug. It may be that all criticism has its origin in this rationalist rejection of the poet's way of being in the world. Faced with uncomprehending or dismissive criticism, the young poet might take heart from something T. S. Eliot once wrote: "Upon giving the matter a little attention, we perceive that criticism, far from being a simple and orderly field of beneficent activity, from which impostors can be readily ejected, is no better than a Sunday park of contending and contentious orators, who have not even arrived at the articulation of their differences." To counter the din of contentious oratory, very little of which will help the writer (or reader) in any useful way, I turn instinctively to the rhetorical question that animates Shakespeare's sonnet sixty-five: "How with this rage shall beauty hold a plea, / Whose action is no stronger than a flower?"

Mark Doty was born in Maryville, Tennessee, in 1953. *Fire to Fire: New and Selected Poems* (HarperCollins, 2008), the most recent of his nine books of poems, won the National Book Award for Poetry in 2008. His work has been honored by the National Book Critics Circle Award, the T. S. Eliot Prize, and the *Los Angeles Times* Book Prize. He has also received a Whiting Writers' Award, fellowships from the Guggenheim and Ingram-Merrill Foundations, an award from the Lila Wallace–Reader's Digest Fund, and a grant from the National Endowment for the Arts. He is the author of five volumes of nonfiction prose, the most recent of which, *Dog Years* (HarperCollins, 2007), won the Israel Fishman Nonfiction Award from the American Library Association. After ten years of teaching at the University of Houston, he joined the faculty at Rutgers University in New Brunswick, New Jersey. He has taught in writing programs around the country, including the University of Iowa Writers' Workshop, New York University, Stanford, Columbia, and Princeton. He is working on two new books, *Deep Lane,* a collection of poems, and a book-length prose meditation on Walt Whitman, desire, and the ecstatic, *What Is the Grass?* He lives in New York City and on the east end of Long Island.

INTRODUCTION

by Mark Doty

◊ ◊ ◊

There was in that same monastery a brother, on whom the gift of writing verses was bestowed by heaven. That sentence, originally in Latin, is from the Venerable Bede, who in 680 composed a history of the English people. It's the subtitle of chapter XXIV, in which Bede tells the story of Caedmon: an origin myth for the art of poetry, and a fable about the nature of inspiration that remains resonant despite the passage of over thirteen hundred years.

Caedmon lived most of his life—Bede tells us he was advanced in years when we enter his story—with no skill in the art of composing verse. When a harp was passed at a party, and each guest expected to contribute a poem or a song, Caedmon would slip out of the room to avoid the humiliation of having no poem to offer his fellows. One evening he'd done just that, and gone out to the stable where he cared for the animals. He lay down to rest, and something marvelous occurred in his dream. "A person appeared to him in his sleep," Bede writes, "and saluting him by his name, said 'Caedmon, sing some song to me.' He answered, 'I cannot sing; for that was the reason why I left the entertainment, and retired to this place because I could not sing.' The other who talked to him replied, 'However, you shall sing.' 'What shall I sing?' rejoined he. 'Sing the beginning of created beings,' said the other."

My guess is that most poets will recognize something of themselves in Caedmon's story. He's an inarticulate man who can't find the right words in the company of his fellows, yet when he's alone—in the company of beasts, which perhaps is where he feels he belongs—something provokes him, someone appears in the dark and says "sing some song to me," or, as Susan Mitchell translates the phrase in a strange and remarkable poem called "Rapture," "Sing me something."

Sing me something is as good a description as I know of what the world or the dark or the visiting spirit seems to say to the poet, as if we were

presented with an imperative, a request, a desire coming from some-
where. Our work is to speak back, but to whom, or to what?

Caedmon's interlocutor has usually been understood as an angel,
and that's the tradition Denise Levertov honors in this beautiful poem
from 1987.

CAEDMON

All others talked as if
talk were a dance.
Clodhopper I, with clumsy feet
would break the gliding ring.
Early I learned to
hunch myself
close by the door:
then when the talk began
I'd wipe my
mouth and wend
unnoticed back to the barn
to be with the warm beasts,
dumb among body sounds
of the simple ones.
I'd see by a twist
of lit rush the motes
of gold moving
from shadow to shadow
slow in the wake
of deep untroubled sighs.
The cows
munched or stirred or were still. I
was at home and lonely,
both in good measure. Until
the sudden angel affrighted me—light effacing
my feeble beam,
a forest of torches, feathers of flame, sparks upflying:
but the cows as before were calm, and nothing was burning,
     nothing but I, as that hand of fire
touched my lips and scorched my tongue
and pulled my voice
        into the ring of the dance.

Levertov's language intensifies in heat as Caedmon's vision kindles: first it's the earthly fire of "the motes / of gold moving / from shadow to shadow" with its calm, almost bovine chain of o's. Then comes the conflagration: "a forest of torches, feathers of flame, sparks upflying." That phrase is dense and satisfying in the mouth, the f's and t's rubbing against one another, the subtle echo of "torches" and "feathers," the double fl's of "flame" and "upflying." Bede himself doesn't say that divine fire touches Caedmon's lips or scorches his tongue, or imply the passive nature of "pulled my voice," as if poetry is something that is done *to* us; that's Levertov's vision, and a compelling one. Bede just says, ". . . he presently began to sing verses to the praise of God . . ." and allows what happened between the beautiful command and Bede's response to remain mysterious.

And Bede doesn't actually say that the one who appears to Caedmon is an angel. He refers to the apparition as *"quiddam"*—Latin for "someone." Someone says, sing me something. Someone, something—the statement couldn't be much more open ended.

To what extent do we understand the process that calls a poem into being? Someone or something comes to us in the dark—literally, or in the darkness of not-knowing—and says "Sing me something." It's the uncovering of what is to be sung, and how, which are not two separate things but an intertwining spiral, like a DNA molecule, that gives the process its tension, frustration, and, at least sometimes, elation.

The someone who speaks may be a vessel of divine fire, as Levertov says, or we might understand him as a shadow self, that side of us which is by nature in darkness, like a side of the moon, and walks a few steps ahead of us into what we don't know yet.

Or we might construe him as the embodied form of absence, a sense of lack within: something incomplete requires our attention.

Perhaps the interlocutory angel is an incarnation of the desire for order, the pressing need to locate and define pattern in the chaos of experience.

Or perhaps he or she is a form of the desire to praise. When faced with something beautiful, Emerson says of poets, they "are not content with admiring, they seek to embody it in new forms."

A little while later in Bede's text, he provides at least a metaphoric understanding of what the poet does with the mysterious prompting, wherever it comes from. The monks tell Caedmon the sacred stories, reciting to him tales from Scripture, and the poet works: "by listening to them and then memorizing it and ruminating over it, like some clean animal chewing the cud, he turned it into the most melodious verse."

Clean animal is delightful. Levertov's Caedmon wanted to dwell

> . . . with the warm beasts,
> dumb among the body sounds
> of the simple ones.

In the barn, he's lulled by their "deep untroubled sighs." Poetry may be the highest use of language, speech with all its multiple powers engaged, but paradoxically it seems to like animal company, the proximity of the purely, wordlessly physical. Perhaps that's another source of the summons: where there are no words, poetry springs into being.

Caedmon dwells among the animals, and presumably he's with them every day, but still it's necessary to sing about them; knowledge must be sung into place, a form of praise and of cartography. A map may show us what we already know, and point us toward what we don't, or reveal the character of what has been obscured by familiarity. To "sing of created beings" is a discipline of attention.

One could also read the silence of animals (not literally, of course, since they make all kinds of noises, but their wordlessness) as a figure for the resistance of all experience to language. Animals are themselves, but they also stand for a realm or register of being that breathes just beneath the surface of the everyday, which is monitored, shaped, and mapped by words; apart from them or beneath them is the creaturely life of the body, the momentous physical life that we are, and are surrounded by every second. I can't think about this without calling to mind George Eliot's remarkable, entirely disruptive aside in *Middlemarch*: "If we had a keen vision and feeling of all ordinary human life, it would be like hearing the grass grow and the squirrel's heart beat, and we should die of that roar which lies on the other side of silence." Poetry is an attempt to move closer to the other side of silence.

I've been talking about the originating impulse of poetry as if it were all interior, a spark arising within obscure regions of the self. But one thing that makes the story of Caedmon satisfyingly complicated is the second instruction the apparition gives to the dreamer. "Sing the beginning of created beings."

And thus complexity and chaos enter into the lyric, since the song that attends to "created beings" can never be pure praise, not if it has allegiance to the real; that requires also lamentation, and outrage, and probably irony as well. Auden addressed the tension between the lyric and the world with characteristic eloquence. He wrote that a "poem should be a verbal earthly paradise, a timeless world of pure play, which gives us delight precisely because of its contrast to our historical existence with all its insoluble problems and inescapable suffering. . . ." But Auden knows all too well that a poem cannot rest there. "At the same time we want a poem to be true . . . and a poet cannot bring us any truth without introducing into his poetry the problematic, the painful, the disorderly, the ugly."

The inner spur, the breath of "inspiration," sometimes is the apprehension of just those things Auden characterizes as the characteristics of truth; that which causes pain may well be the spur which leads the poet to begin. The inner voice and the social world are in endless dialogue; like form and content, it can—and should—be difficult to tease the two apart.

So far you'd have no reason to think this essay an introduction to an anthology. This is a deliberate choice. The twenty-four distinguished poets who've edited one of these collections before have done a bang-up job of introducing them, and there's little for me to add that's specific to the project itself.

But a few things must be said.

First, the seventy-five poems I've placed before you here are the ones that engaged me most during a year of reading a great many poems. "Best" is problematic, if unavoidable; poetry is not an Olympic competition in which there are a few coveted places at the top. Differences in the range of modes, the means of speaking, are fundamentally of value, and a wide and various field of activity is much to be preferred over a pyramidal scheme in which only a few examples can shine at the pinnacle. And even if I believed in such a thing, how would I know? The clouded vision of the present will shift, in time, whether toward clarity or toward some other kind of cloudedness. History will, inevitably, make choices among the poems of our moment, and history will revise those choices in time, if indeed there's anyone around to read or construct canons in a few hundred years. Meanwhile, I'm happy that a range of voices is included here, as well as poems that appeared in trade magazines and in online-only journals, publications with legions of readers or a handful. Hooray for that. And the poets here are well known indeed or just setting out, or somewhere in between; they have umpteen books or no book at all.

Second, I should acknowledge the obvious, that I read (and read and read) through the filters of my own taste, which a project like this inevitably foregrounds. Anthology-making is, at least on one level, a form of self-portraiture. This book might well be called *Seventy-Five Poems Mark Likes,* but who'd buy that? And "likes" is too slight— believes in? Wishes to keep, to dwell within? It's plain that I favor a certain disciplined richness of language, a considered relation between restraint and gorgeousness. And I'm drawn to poems that push against the boundaries of what is accepted as real, reaching into the life of the spirit, past the boundaries of the known and acknowledged toward what's harder to name. I'll side with Whitman, as Robert Hass does in his poem "Consciousness":

> . . . not interested, he said, in
> the people who need to say that we all die and life is a suck
> and a sell and two plus two is four and nothing left over.

Let the poem's allegiance be to what's hardest to name.

Third, I want to publicly take off my hat to David Lehman, who has energetically and efficiently (now I know just *how* efficiently) guided the series he initiated through twenty-five years of publication. A quarter century of editorship and advocacy represents serious literary heroism, a profound commitment to the art—and David has been remarkably catholic in his practices, choosing a range of guest editors, pointing them quietly toward his own favorites but also getting out of his guests' way while managing to gently shepherd us along when we linger by the side of the path. This collection represents a labor of love for me (I read more literary magazines more systematically than I ever have before, enjoying the feeling of pouring myself into what flooded my mailbox) and a huge amount of work for David, his publisher, and their supporting staff. To sustain this all this time, without showing any signs of fatigue or flagging interest—well, it's an extraordinary contribution to the art, and to our understanding of what American poetry is at this moment.

We could also say that phantom who appears to the poet, summoning words, is some premonition or anticipation of the reader—who turns to poetry in order to find some music that echoes what we can't say, to read the inscription of our common lot, to be challenged and engaged, to be less alone, to be startled awake.

All right, I hope you'll say, opening this book, sing me something.

(A note of gratitude to Alex Duym, for material concerning Caedmon and his context. And to Alexander Hadel, for practically everything else.)

THE
BEST
AMERICAN
POETRY
2012

◊ ◊ ◊

Terminal Nostalgia

◇   ◇   ◇

The music of my youth was much better
Than the music of yours. So was the weather.

Before Columbus came, eagle feathers
Detached themselves for us. So did the weather.

During war, the country fought together
Against all evil. So did the weather.

The cattle were happy to be leather
And made shoes that fit. So did the weather.

Before Columbus came, eagle feathers
Were larger than eagles. So was the weather.

Every ball game was a double-header.
Mickey Mantle was sober. So was the weather.

Before Adam and Eve, an Irish Setter
Played fetch with God. So did the weather.

Before Columbus came, eagle feathers
Married Indians. So did the weather.

Indians were neither loaners nor debtors.
Salmon was our money. So was the weather.

Back then, people wrote gorgeous letters
And read more poetry. So did the weather.

On all issues, there was only one dissenter,
But we loved him, too. So did the weather.

Before Columbus came, eagle feathers
Gave birth to eagles. So did the weather.

We all apprenticed to wise old mentors
And meditated for days. So did the weather.

We were guitar-players and inventors
Of minor chords and antibiotics. So was the weather.

Every person lived near the city center
And had the same income. So did the weather.

Before Columbus, eagle feathers
Lived in the moment. So did the weather.

from *Green Mountains Review*

Receipt: Midway Entertainment Presents

◊ ◊ ◊

Two kinds of fair: carnie and perambulator
of the local: shiny peppers on paper plates

and buttercream silk goats: Lizabet & Hope
among the floral displays gone south:

please enter again, this was very strong,
next year. A staged race of pigs in felt coats:

picked out in red, green, blue around a track,
shivering a ring of fat kids used to this

easy choice: commercial, delicious
fries or the sad white bread of the VFW barbeque.

Right among the sloe-eyed dirty cow hose-down,
a tired show horse to pet. Sort of oversold

at the 5 buck K9 demonstration; 4H got a thousand
for a rough old hog in red second-place satin.

Dad explains: *Claire's photos won because*
Claire's photos were best. It's that fair, the big gray

hair of a tufted chicken, the mascaraed rabbit that
no one gets are supposed to mold you from the fantastic

to the rational: *I would like to thank God for this medal.*
Down at the midway end past the chainsaw bears,

the Old People Tap Dance Show, and the bee man
in the ag tent, madly pointing at the holes

in his rigged up hive, Mom inspects busted latches
and the blanks between boards and wires,

the scuffed blue of the Tilt-A-Whirl's shelf; on which
is the kind of fair you could get used to;

all places being equal to the blast of bad rock
and the rust metal floor; a flat coke no one would want;

ordinary; just one boy's or one girl's sweaty hands
on offer, unspecial.

from *Seneca Review*

Accounts

◇   ◇   ◇

for Brian Keating

Light was on its way
from nothing
to nowhere.

Light was all business

   Light was full speed

when it got interrupted.

Interrupted by what?

When it got tangled up
and broke
into opposite

   broke into brand-new things.

   What kinds of things?

   Drinking Cup

     "Thinking of you!
          Convenience Valet"

How could speed take shape?

Hush!
Do you want me to start over?

The fading laser pulse

    Information describing the fading laser pulse

is stored

    is encoded

in the spin states
of atoms.

God
is balancing his checkbook

    God is encrypting his account.

This is taking forever!

from *Poetry*

For Furious Nursing Baby

◇　◇　◇

Frothy and pink as a rabid pig you—
a mauler—
　　　　　　a lunatic stricken with

a madness induced by flesh—
　　　　　　squeeze my skin
until blotched nicked. Your fingernails

are jagged
　　　and mouth-slick. Pinprick scabs
　　　jewel my breasts.
　　　　　　　　Your tongue
your wisest muscle
　　　is the wet engine
　　　　　　　　of discontent.
It self-fastens by a purse-bead of spit

while your elegant hands
　　　　　　　flail conducting
orchestral milk
　　　and sometimes prime the pump.

Nipple in mouth
　　　　　　　nipple in hand
you have your cake and eat it too.

Then when wrenched
         loose you'll eat sorrow loss—
                  one flexed hand twists
as you open your mouth
           to eat your fist.

from *The Cincinnati Review*

Outside

◇ ◇ ◇

Stevie lives in a silo.
A silo lives where, mostly, Stevie is
or is not. Tipped over—a hollow vein.
The silo, I mean. For here home is out
there on the grass. If you want a drink or wash
your hands, just dip into that trunk, hot and cold
running branches feeding down. It's startling.
But sense is startling, too. See how those boots
flip skyward? Tongues lapping up dew on his
mâché dandelions. This is Stevie's dream

miniacreage on the family's old spread.
He's all spread out; he's humming when he makes
a working thing—he won't let you inside.
"So," he says. Today he's stacked two propane
tanks and ovens—two-burners—under a
red maple, and when you open a door
there's mismatched silver and hatchets and things
he's made to eat *and* art with. Studio
as wherever-you're-itching-at-the-time:
boards with big nails banged in and from the nails

hang gourds, baby-sized cups speckled yellow
(is that old egg?), a hundred kinds of who
knows what, the center being where you are
and are not. "I stay dry," he says. "No bugs."
Says, "Why do walls want windows?" He's put glass
around his trees instead, head-high, to look
at trees from outside out. One chair, sleeping bag

—what he keeps inside the wild corn bin—
plus a getaway, by which he means a tunnel.
"Oh oh," he says, "they coming." He can worm

his way all the way to the apple trees,
he trenched it out last fall, and lights the route
with flashlights and tinfoil clipped to clothesline.
That's a trip. And that's a curvy planter full
of nursery nipples and hand-dipped Ken dolls.
If you want to see an art made wholly
in an outside mind, come see Stevie's crib.
That's his ten-foot pink polyvinyl penis
teeter-totter beside the birdcage
for potatoes. "Take a ride," he says. All eyes—.

from *The Southern Review*

Child Holding Potato

◇ ◇ ◇

When my sister got her diagnosis,
I bought an airplane ticket

but to another city, where I stared
at paintings that seemed victorious

in their relation to time:
the beech from two hundred years ago,

its trunk a palette of mud
and gilt; the man with olive-black

gloves, the sky behind him
a glacier of blue light. In their calm

landscapes, the saints. Still dripping
the garden's dew, the bouquets.

Holding the rough gold orb
of a potato, the Child cradled

by the glowing Madonna. Then,
the paintings I looked at the longest:

the bowls of plums and peaches,
the lemons, the pomegranates

like red earths. In my mouth,
the raw starch. In my mouth, the dirt.

from *Memorious*

At the End of Life, a Secret

◇ ◇ ◇

Everything measured. A man twists
a tuft of your hair out for no reason
other than you are naked before him
and he is bored. Moments ago he was
weighing your gallbladder, and then
he was staring at the empty space where
your lungs were. Even dead, we still say
you are an organ donor, as if something
other than taxes outlasts death. Your feet
are regular feet. Two of them,
and there is no mark to suggest you were
an expert mathematician, that you were
the first runner-up in debate championships,
1956, Tapioca, Illinois. From the time your body
was carted before him, to the time your
dead body is being sent to the coffin,
every pound is accounted for, except 22 grams.
The man is a praying man & has figured
what it means. He says this is the soul, finally,
after the breath has gone. The soul: less than
4,000 dollars' worth of crack—22 grams—
all that moves you through this world.

from *New England Review*

Of His Bones Are Coral Made

◊   ◊   ◊

He still trolled books, films, gossip, his own
past, searching not just for

ideas that dissect the mountain that

in his early old age he is almost convinced
cannot be dissected:

he searched for stories:

stories the pattern of whose
knot dimly traces the pattern of his own:

what is intolerable in

the world, which is to say
intolerable in himself, ingested, digested:

the stories that

haunt each of us, for each of us
rip open the mountain.

*

the creature smothered in death clothes

dragging into the forest
bodies he killed to make meaning

the woman who found that she

to her bewilderment and horror
had a body

*

As if certain algae

that keep islands of skeletons
alive, that make living rock from

trash, from carcasses left behind by others,

as if algae
were to produce out of

themselves and what they most fear

the detritus over whose
kingdom they preside: the burning

fountain is the imagination

within us that ingests and by its
devouring generates

what is most antithetical to itself:

it returns the intolerable as
brilliant dream, visible, opaque,

teasing analysis:

makes from what you find hardest to
swallow, most indigestible, your food.

from *Salmagundi*

Pill

◊ ◊ ◊

Say you are high all the time save those moments
you take a sobriety tablet and so descend
the nerves of the heart, thinking straight,

they call it, as if the mind were an arrow
shot from the eye into the eyes of others,
the ones you wronged, the ones you never knew

you love or do not love, the black fathoms
of their pupils deepening as your eyes close.
And sure it hurts, how something dead walks out

your sleep, how it goes from blue to red
like blood. And yet the stuff keeps calling you
in a father's voice. You loved your father,

so it's more than bitter seeds you swallow.
It's quiet pleasure within the limitations
of one life, until the great space of a day

gets wider, brighter, as if you were slipping
into summer with its giant measures
of desire, the way just sitting makes it rise.

And yes, with each dose comes the gravity
and boredom, the slow crush of August heat,
though you are learning to live here, in a town

with one good street to speak of, one flock of trees
to storm the night. In time you are addicted.
And it takes more of the drug to get you back

to the world, where morning swallows flit
in last night's rain. In time you tell yourself
you are the age you are: the little pains

inside your arms, your legs, they are just that:
the pinch that says you are not asleep,
that the compulsion you feel is the pull

of the planet you walk, alone. And the dawn,
however deep you breathe, is everyone's now,
everyone's breath in the sky above you,

everyone's sun aching into layers
of mist, spitting fire in the eye,
its one black star dissolving, like a pill.

from *Colorado Review*

Notre Dame

◊   ◊   ◊

I was staying in an apartment near Notre Dame.
There was a park for the kids to play.
Roller skaters in front of the cathedral in the evening, and my older son joined in.
We shared the floor of the apartment.
Too many family members of mine sleeping there.
One morning I woke up and in the instant
Before my full vision came back I saw or apprehended or felt or however
You want to call that almost-seeing that happens—
Two angels hovering: one was male and one was female.
They were there to be with my younger son, protecting him or visiting.
The male especially was there to care for him.
They were checking on him as he slept.
I had interrupted by seeing them and so they had to leave.
In fact, the male angel stayed maybe a moment too long
And the female was communicating this message like, "Hurry up, come on!"
It was known to me that I wasn't supposed to see them.
They were annoyed with me.
After waking, fully, and lying on the floor before everyone else stirred,
My mind wandered over to Notre Dame:
My parents made a pilgrimage every year, just to be near it.
I loved the thoughtful gargoyle up at the top.
Inside the human souls came to visit out of pain or tourism
Or death approaching, or craving union,
Out of loneliness and sickness. Out of boredom.
Candles burned their prayers for someone.
What had I seen? Anything? You always doubt something like that.
How could that be real? And yet
It was a terrible summer, and it required angels, real or dreamed,
With my father losing his mind, getting lost;

My mother losing the ability to walk,
A sister comforting me as I lamented and talked
My sad story while our children played together at the playground
At the Tuileries. Later, when I could laugh again
And tell the summer as a tale, I said that
It's sad to walk around the Seine when you are getting divorced while everyone else
Is kissing and filming their honeymoons or new loves. Even
My husband, after we got back together, laughed at that.
Because he, too, had been heartsick on another part of the planet.

from *The American Poetry Review*

ANNE CARSON

Sonnet of Exemplary Sentences From the Chapter Pertaining to the Nature of Pronouns in Emile Benveniste's Problems in General Linguistics (Paris 1966)

◇　◇　◇

This time I forgive you but I shall not forgive you again.
I observe that he forgives you but he will not forgive you again.
Although I eat this fish I don't know its name.
Spirits watch over the soul of course.
I suppose and I presume.
I pose and I resume.
I suppose I have a horse.
How in the world can you afford this house I said and she said

I had a good divorce.
Strangers are warned that here there is a fierce, fast dog.
Whores have no business getting lost in the fog.
Is it to your ears or your soul that my voice is intolerable?
Whether Florinda lays a hand on his knee or his voluble, he pleads a headache
and the narrator concludes, *The problem is insoluble.*

from *The Nation*

Dorothy Wordsworth

◊   ◊   ◊

The daffodils can go fuck themselves.
I'm tired of their crowds, yellow rantings
about the spastic sun that shines and shines
and shines. How are they any different

from me? I, too, have a big messy head
on a fragile stalk. I spin with the wind.
I flower and don't apologize. There's nothing
funny about good weather. Oh, spring again,

the critics nod. They know the old joy,
that wakeful quotidian, the dark plot
of future growing things, each one
labeled *Narcissus nobilis* or *Jennifer Chang*.

If I died falling from a helicopter, then
this would be an important poem. Then
the ex-boyfriends would swim to shore
declaiming their knowledge of my bulbous

youth. O, Flower, one said, why aren't you
meat? But I won't be another bashful shank.
The tulips have their nervous joie-de-vivre,
the lilacs their taunt. Fractious petals, stop

interrupting my poem with boring beauty.
All the boys are in the field gnawing raw

bones of ambition and calling it ardor. Who
the hell are they? This is a poem about war.

from *The Nation*

Sparrow

◇ ◇ ◇

St. John of the Cross

On the oil spot,
in the Municipal Parking Garage, I am a garden
closed up
       & a fountain sealed. In the folds of my habit;
in the wings of my rib cage;
I hold nothingness like a black jewel.

Fountain of Self, Fountain of the Interior.
I strip to my skin. Dark clouds illuminate me.
Moths fly around;
       I am puzzled by the light.

Withdraw your eyes. These steel cables are flesh.
This elevator's silver car is holy.

And the floor numbers—strung up like lanterns
on the boat of the dead.

I'm half-life. I'm already words
& the Sparrow.
       Listen for me in your throat when I'm gone.

from *The Cincinnati Review*

BASIC

◇   ◇   ◇

This program is designed to move a white line
from one side of the screen to the other.

This program is not too hard, but it has
a sad ending and that makes people cry.

This program is designed to make people cry
and step away when they are finished.

In one variation the line moves diagonally
up and in another diagonally down.

This makes people cry differently,
diagonally. A whole room of people

crying in response to this program's
variations results in beautiful music.

This program is designed to make such
beautiful music that it feels like at last

they have allowed you to take the good canoe
into the lake of your own choosing

and above you the sky exposes one
or two real eagles, the water

warm or marked with stones,
however you like it, blue.

from *The New Yorker*

HENRI COLE

Broom

◇   ◇   ◇

A starkly lighted room with a tangy iron odor;

a subterranean dankness; a metal showerhead hanging from the ceiling;

a scalpel, a trocar, a pump; a white marble table; a naked, wrinkled

body faceup on a sheet, with scrubbed skin, clean nails,

and shampooed hair; its mouth sewn shut, with posed lips,

its limbs massaged, its arteries drained, its stomach and intestines emptied;

a pale blue sweater, artificial pearls, lipstick, and rouge;

hands that once opened, closed, rolled, unrolled, rerolled, folded, unfolded,

turned, and returned, as if breathing silver, unselfing themselves now

(very painful); hands that once tore open, rended, ripped,

served, sewed, and stroked (very loving), pushing and butting now

with all their strength as their physiognomy fills with firming fluid;

hands once raucous, sublime, quotidian—now strange, cruel, neat;

hands that once chased me gruesomely with a broom, then brushed my hair.

from *The Threepenny Review*

Delivery

◇   ◇   ◇

Moon moving in the upper window,
shadow of the pen in my hand on the page—
I keep wishing that the news of my death

will be delivered by a little wooden truck
or a child's drawing of a truck
featuring the long rectangular box of the trailer,

with some lettering on the side,
then the protruding cab, the ovoid wheels,
maybe the inscrutable profile of a driver,

and of course puffs of white smoke
issuing from the tail pipe, drawn like flowers
and similar in their expression to the clouds in the sky only smaller.

from *Subtropics*

More Than Twice, More Than I Can Count

◊   ◊   ◊

Down here, with my long wait for wings to grow
I'm slow accepting the stars' chart for me,
the blind track written in my sky at birth.
I have my glimpses, terrible and deep,
moments when I can see a kind of plan,
and more than twice tracing the lineaments
in one of the live oaks in City Park
New Orleans legend says were born with Christ,
or in the face of a beautiful child
or yes—why not say it—a flowering light
hibiscus blossoms open and then close
in sunlight's entrance, exit through the cloud—
say it: I've seen, head-on the face of God
cracked, fractured, splintered, never what I want
but mine, nevertheless and, yes, these wings'
sutures, at more than half a century
with me almost immeasurable in light,
itch and lift me here where blue ground meets sky.
For a few seconds I am only blue.
I have my little time in Paradise.

from *Harvard Review*

To the Angelbeast

◇   ◇   ◇

for Arthur Russell

All that glitters isn't music.

Once, hidden in tall grass,
I tossed fistfuls of dirt into the air:
doe after doe of leaping.

You said it was nothing
but a trick of the light. Gold
curves. Gold scarves.

Am I not your animal?

You'd wait in the orchard for hours
to watch a deer
break from the shadows.

You said it was like lifting a cello
out of its black case.

from *Poetry*

Back Matter

◇   ◇   ◇

Semantics 2.0,
Daughter, still, of absurdities,
I like "street-talker" now. Yes, please.
Breathless with ghetto woe
(". . . and his mama cried") I'd call
Me too American, too black,
Too Negro dialect. My back
Is to your front. I'm all
Set with my Nikes on.

*

Back: as in "go," sound on the tongue
Articulated, clean, clearly hung
In the aft of the mouth.

*

                    Back: dawn
As near is to December. I
Walk in the flakes as doctors try
To drink their coffee, yawn
In mittened hands while they
Cross MLK and I decide
To take the hill, walk farther, ride
It out this Saturday,
Cold, cocked, nothing.

                    And Back:

Pertaining to support; to cause
To move backward; hems, haws,
But strength, effort; no lack-
Luster labor.

*

     I put
My back into it, start to sweat
And feel the Sempiternam, wet,
There in the skin afoot,
All itchy, from the needle
(Wednesday's fresh ink). I turn and head
For red EMERGENCY—

               hot bed,

A microcosm, beetle
Of Cincinnati streets
Where pigs have got a man spread-eagle,
Cuffed to a gurney with the legal
Miranda said, the beats

Of EKGs, the blood
Of GS to the chest,
STAT angiectomy,

            last rites,
Urban Gethsemane, left bites
Of Jell-O.

*

         Back: to rest;
Arrears or overdue;
Belonging to the past like back
In the day.

*

     The once-crazy could crack—

*

The defending player who,
Behind the other players, makes
First contact—

*

      Streets are talking, rakes
Catcalling, and the new
Sky's crisp as all the streams
Of frozen runoff.
         There's no help
For me, just voices: barest yelp,
Incessant chatter, screams;

It's my emergency,
My good-luck charm, my fetish carved
In brain waves; and, I'm fucking starved
For more synecdoche—

More forms: the water-trickle
When it melts in spring, the med(evac!),
A glass door sliding off its track—
A million worlds to tickle
My fancy.
        "Ma'am, you next?"

I leave the hospital and walk
For milk, though I need none. I stalk
A flying flier, text
Muddied by snow and now
Unreadable.

*

Back is the how
You know where you have been; the Tao;
"What up"; instead of "ciao,"
"Peace"; "One"; a vision too
Damn visible in memory.

*

32

Only I have to listen. See?
I'm still the jigaboo.

Don't see me as I butt
In highs and lows and every nome
And phoneme while on my way home
To lay back in the cut.

from *Barrow Street*

STEPHEN DUNN

The Imagined

◊　◊　◊

If the imagined woman makes the real woman
seem bare-boned, hardly existent, lacking in
gracefulness and intellect and pulchritude,
and if you come to realize the imagined woman
can only satisfy your imagination, whereas
the real woman with all her limitations
can often make you feel good, how, in spite
of knowing this, does the imagined woman
keep getting into your bedroom, and joining you
at dinner, why is it that you always bring her along
on vacations when the real woman is shopping,
or figuring the best way to the museum?

And if the real woman

has an imagined man, as she must, someone
probably with her at this very moment, in fact
doing and saying everything she's ever wanted,
would you want to know that he slips in
to her life every day from a secret doorway
she's made for him, that he's present even when
you're eating your omelette at breakfast,
or do you prefer how she goes about the house
as she does, as if there were just the two of you?

Isn't her silence, finally, loving? And yours
not entirely self-serving? Hasn't the time come,

        once again, not to talk about it?

from *The New Yorker*

A Story Begins

◇   ◇   ◇

The same as other stories, but we follow along in case something different might happen.

Just one different thing. It leads us to a ledge and pushes us over.

Every story has a climax in a way life doesn't.

It puts us back where it found us. It opens our eyes which weren't closed, but felt that way because what we saw was happening inside the story.

We are the excess of the story—that which it cannot contain.

Washed ashore.

What was the story about?

I can't remember. A dwindling, dim-witted tribe.

Every month when the moon was full, they'd sacrifice another virgin, but could never figure out why the crops still wouldn't grow.

from *New American Writing*

Spirit in the Dark

◇   ◇   ◇

What to make of the night we sat up late,
Listening to Beethoven's *Ninth*

In that otherwise darkened apartment?
The New York Philharmonic

Was gathering together the fragments
At the fourth movement's start—

Momentum they'd ride like a wave
Through the fanfare and final chorus—

When we felt something else enter the air,
A front in the weather of the room.

It sat us upright on the edge of our chairs
While it tracked toward the record

And hung suspended for a measure or two
Above the still point of the stylus.

Then, just as steadily, it withdrew,
A patch of fog that had been burned off . . .

The look the dead raised on your face
Must have been the same on my own.

"What was that?" our expressions asked.
Decades later, I'd still like to know.

And what changes, if any, were played
Upon us? And did any of them take?

"Be embraced," the chorus sang,
And then the crescendo and kettledrums,

The whole *Ninth* welling before us
Before fading as well from the room.

from *Prairie Schooner*

Self-Portrait with No Internal Navigation

◊   ◊   ◊

Have you ever been arrested? The pigeon arrests me.
No, not the wing but the sturdy round body & the sheen
of the throat, like the interior of a snail's shell or the bruise
of spring—think of the lilac blistered with blossoms,
of the burned grouse moor's sudden eruption into heather—
a beauty we expect only from what's broken. Have you ever
gone too far? Last week, I overshot the same junction twice
along a simple stretch of country road. And Philippe Petit
crossed eight times between The Towers. This is what
the officers at the station told him later when he was through.
He had no idea how long he'd hovered, how many times
he reversed himself, passing onto something almost
like earth beyond the far guy-wire, only to pivot back again—
lying down even, one leg dangling—above loose, swaying
space. I worry about the pigeons beginning today to roost
on the ferry that shuttles back & forth between two capes.
A pair of pigeons mates for a lifetime, produces, at most,
two squabs each year. They have chosen this spot because,
centuries ago, they were domestic—the words are *coop*
& *columbarium*—because they still love, past reason,
the swift tides of our voices, are drawn to the chattering crew
even as it swats at them now with brooms & paints
the sooty pipes above the car deck with a chemical tar
concocted to burn the birds' feet. Once my husband chose
to step out into open air. He fell but was somehow returned
to me. Feral cousin of the carrier & racer, the rock dove steers

with a certainty we cannot imagine. Still, what if one flies
into the marsh for reeds for the nest just as the boat sets sail?
How will it know to simply sit & wait? And what of the panic
of the one departed? The one who has left without leaving.

from *Mead: The Magazine of Literature and Libations*

Helianthus annuus
(Sunflower)

◇　◇　◇

Irrational you may be, in the way

That mathematicians mean it. But you're all
About efficiencies, optimizations.

From apex to primordia, you spiral
Into control, *girasole*, you flower
Of the golden mean, the gyre, the twist, the curve.

Triumph of coincidence, master of packing
Density, attentiveness to detail.
And all this from a flower no one planted,
Arisen from last year's spillage from the birdhouse,
Two thousand seeds for the one that engendered you.

Weary of time? I think not. Object lesson
For adepts of the trigonometries
Of Fibonacci—you *are* time, a living
Sundial, tireless tracker of the light's
Trajectory. You know, you flaming thing,
You august standard-bearer for the skies
In their last and greatest clarity before
The cloudy season, you know there is nothing

Random in the way a space is filled.
Nothing ever doesn't make sense. We

Can do the math: each thing will always be
The sum of things that came before it. Write
This message in the borders of the garden:
Phi, the symbol of the mean you mean,
The disc atop the slim stalk. Yes, and fie,
By the way, on any and all who'd think to call
You weary of time, who'd wrongly reify
Those bending rays, that reverent chin-to-chest
Kowtow. You know of mortal gravity,
Sun-worshipper, you pythia of pith
And oil, you oracle of harmony,
Order and reason. Of course you bow to it.

from *New England Review*

One Train's Survival Depends on the Other Derailed

◊   ◊   ◊

after Susan Mitchell

In a bar in Chicago like a bar in New York, the anthems hang
in the jukebox air: *I Will Survive, Maybe This Time,*

the bartender's nipple ring catching the discoball's shrapnel light,
on a night which begins in wan November, dancing

with a chestnut-haired Aries, the scorch of us hurtling like a train
I want to step in front of. He takes my hand when we leave the bar,

we walk a greasy sidewalk to a private courtyard, he kisses me
and the world goes magnolia, quick white flash back

to the garden I hid in as a boy, interred in a noiseless mangle,
the tree's opalescent sepals masking my upturned face

as I imagine a real life GI Joe come to the rescue, smiling down
into the plot, shovel in hand. He kisses me on a night

so rinsed in purity it begs for its own ending.
The night's begging lodged in me. We're parallel trains

lurching forward, jaunting windows jaggedly aligned.
Don't love the train, it craves to be emptied.

When we part, a February starfield blooming above us
in the dead of winter, he's wiping the kiss off his lips.

Don't miss me, he says, hailing a cab, paying the driver,
saying goodbye with a sterile hug. I miss the stars,

which had leaned in close. In November, I could die
happy, his saliva drying on my neck, the breeze

violining its song along the sloped avenue.
The song expires on the radio of an overheated car

speeding eastward into the night after the secret courtyard,
after the snow lowered its gentle hammer on the skulls

of lovers, the night I know in my sudden blood
I am going to kill myself. Don't miss me,

the discoball moon says to the lake. Don't miss me
says a boy to the plastic partition, the snow melting

down his face in tracks, in February, on a night
stricken at last of starlight, shocked dumb,

night with its shovel and its covering dark.

from *New England Review*

The Rose Has Teeth

◇ ◇ ◇

after Matmos & M. Zapruder

I was trying to play the twelve-bar blues with two bars.
I was trying to fill the room with a shocked and awkward color,
I was trying to limber your shuffle, the muscle wired to muscle.
I wanted to be a lucid hammer. I was trying to play
like the first mechanic asked to repair the first automobile.
Once, Piano, every man-made song could fit in your mouth.
But I was trying to play Burial's "Ghost Hardware."
I was trying to play "Steam and Sequins for Larry Levan"
without the artificial bells and smoke. I was trying to play
the sound of applause by trying to play the sound of rain.
I was trying to mimic the stain on a bed, the sound
of a woman's soft, contracting bellow, the answer to who I am.
Before I trust the god who makes me rot, I trust you, Piano.
Something deathless fills your wood. Because I wanted to be
invisible, I was trying to play like a woman blacker
than an unpaid light bill, like a white boy lost in the snow.
I wanted to be a ghost because the skull is just a few holes
covered in meat. The skin has no teeth. I was trying to play
the sound of a shattered window. I was trying to play what I felt
singing in the mirror as a boy. I was trying to play what I overheard:
the old questions, the hunger, the rattle of spines. The body
that only loves what it can touch always turns to dust.
What would a mother feel if her child sang "Sometimes I Feel
Like a Motherless Child" too beautifully? A hole has no teeth.
A bird has no teeth. But you got teeth, Piano. You make me high.
You make me dance as only a sail can dance its ragged assailable

dance. You make me believe there is good in me.
I was trying to play "California Dreaming" with José Feliciano's
warble. I was trying to play it the way George Benson played it
on the guitar his daddy made him at the end of the war. My lady,
she dreams of Chicago. I was trying to play "Mouhamadou Bamba"
like a band of Africans named after a tree. A tree has no teeth.
A horn has no teeth. Don't chew, Piano. Don't chew, sing to me
you fine-ass lounging harp. You fancy engine doing other people's
work. I was trying to play the sound of an empty house
because that's how I get by when the darkness in my body
starts to bleed. I was trying to play "Autumn Leaves"
because that's what my lady's falling dress sounds like to me.
Before you, Piano, I was just a rap of knuckles on the sill. I am filled
with the sound of her breathing and only you can bring it out of me.

from *Tin House*

Collision

◊   ◊   ◊

Away in the eyefar
nightrise over the sapwood, and one likes
under hooves the heatfeel after sun flees, heat stays on this
smooth to the hoof hardpan, part trail
part saltlick now as snowlast moults back
into the sapwood
to yard and rot
and one sees moonrise mounding
over a groundswell, but too soon and swifter
like never the moon one knows, no moon at all,
two moons fawned, both small, too hot, they
come with a growling and
hold one fast, so chafing for flight
but what, what, what, what
wondering——

and one can't move and can't although one
knows from backdays, eared and glimpsed
through sapwood   budwood   cracklewood   bonewood
flashes of this same Wolfing
                              now upon one, still
stalls the hooves on the saltlick and the eyebright
creature squeals   afraid?——and one somehow
uphoofed in a bound not chosen high as if to flee with no
trying, no feeling, fallen   flankflat, fawnlike
eyes above in the eyefar closing small
with the world

                    and now from the stopped thing

comes what   its cub?   legged up on its hinds,
kneels low to touch, but in that awful
touch, no feel   no fear to feel
no at all—

from *The Literary Review*

Moaning Action at the Gas Pump

◊   ◊   ◊

. . . in the tragic world, all moaning tends to consider itself music.
Nicole Loraux

Soon it will be necessary to start a behavior of moaning outdoors when pumping gas . . . That capital **S** is a sort of gas nozzle. Pulling up, beginning a low moaning action, pulling a deep choral moan with cracks up through the body, the crude through the cracks of sea & earth, pulling neurotransmitters glutamate, acetylcholine, & others across chasms in the nervous system, into the larynx until the sound acts by itself. *Customer copy, look us in the eye.* So we shred the song to continue. Meaning morning moaning mourning. i am able to complete 34 moans by the time i've filled half the tank. City-states outlawed open wailing because it was not good for democracy, but you will merely be embarrassed even if you drive a hybrid. Please be embarrassed. Please.

Inside the pump, you can hear a bird, a screech-covered *Pelecanus occidentalis* lugged out of the Gulf with 4 million tons of the used booms in non-leakable plastic, 13 million tons of liquid in nonleakable plastic 5 miles up the road—their **5** has a leak in it by the way—the moan fans out as you put your head down on the hood of your car; please moan though the other drivers are staring. Squeak, there are other animals inside the pump, the great manatee—*Trichechus manatus*—you've seen it float like a rug that has something wrapped in it among grasses that will not return. ***eeeoooiieeooooouuuuu,*** this moan won't be the same mammal but is a democracy with no false knowledge, the sounds pushed to the edge of a painting, globs of oil floating to shores of salt-marshes. The broadcaster says the globs "look like peanut butter," wanting to sound lovable so we can begin to feel friendly about them. Ever since 3 wars ago the moan meeting other moans & you ask how to get over it . . . is it like Gilgamesh & Enkidu, David & Absolom, like Isis & Osiris, like Ishmael & history, is it like Hecuba & her kids, Cassandra who did not drive, is it like Mary, like Antigone who could barely lift the body to bury it, probably you don't you don't have to probably you don't have to get over it—

from *Gulf Coast*

In a Kitchen Where Mushrooms Were Washed

◊   ◊   ◊

In a kitchen where mushrooms were washed,
the mushroom scent lingers.

As the sea must keep for a long time the scent of the whale.

As a person who's once loved completely,
a country once conquered,
does not release that stunned knowledge.

They must want to be found, those strange-shaped, rising morels,
clownish puffballs.

Lichens have served as a lamp wick.
Clean-burning coconuts, olives.
Dried salmon, sheep fat, a carcass of petrel set blazing:
light that is fume and abradement.

Unburnable mushrooms are other.
They darken the air they come into.

Theirs the scent of having been traveled, been taken.

from *Ploughshares*

A Proposed Curriculum Change

◇　◇　◇

Dear Mrs Masters,
It's happened *again*!
    and the whole Fifth-Grade Class is upset
(which is why we're *writing* again: you told us
    to tell you when "*anything* related to
school" upsets the class,
                so now we're telling).
                You see, just last week,
thanks to Mr Lee's
    connections (that's what he calls the friends
who do him favors), our Fifth-Grade Science Class,
    all twelve, until the Klein twins got mumps,
—together, of course—
               and had to stay home,
               so we invited
Mike Rahn and Clark Taft,
    the two smartest kids in the Fourth-Grade,
to come instead, since Mr Lee had specified
    there would be twelve students visiting
the Sandusky Labs
              for our winter-term
              science field trip, and
no one wants to see
    two favors go to waste. Dinny—that's
Mr Lee: he *asked* us all to call him that,
    and now he's the one teacher at school

we're on first-name, or
maybe nick-name terms
with . . . whom. Anyway,
Dinny has this friend Mr Morton
who works in the Labs (he told us right away,
"Call me Mort, everyone does"—first names
must be a sort of
code for Scientists),
on the development
of cancerous tumors that he trained
to grow in mice (*induced* was the word he used).
When he offered to show us how
his experiment
was coming along,
Lucy Wensley asked
"Mr Mort" if he could tell one mouse
from the next: "Do you ever see something
individual about a mouse—
some particular
mouse you're working on?"
(Lucy sometimes brings
her pet guinea-pig to school with her,
so of course she'd ask a thing like that.)
Her question really surprised Mort, but
maybe what he said
was a good answer;
after a moment
he told this story: last week he had
to kill a mouse with a newborn litter, and
to save her young, gave them to another
mouse to bring them up
with her own; and when
that experiment
worked, he gave that foster-mother mouse
another litter of newborn young, to see
what she would do. At first all went well:
the new babies were
fat and already
growing fur, though still

blind—and then one night she ate them all! . . .
Not just Lucy but our whole Class, including
    the two Fourth-Graders, listened without
                  saying anything.
                  Nobody moved. Mort
opened the lab door,
    saying "Boys and girls, please come with me"
and the spell was broken. But Mrs Masters,
    no one has forgotten Mort's story.
                  Over and over
                  in Dinny's classes
we've learned this lesson:
    In the Animal World—and aren't we
animals too?—mothers and fathers go
    after their young, all shapes and sizes,
                  pigs in model farms,
                  Komodo dragons,
and now even mice!
    Maybe our own parents will eat *us*
eventually—they may have eaten us
    already, and the rest of our life
                  is just the process
                  of their digestion.
That's not our life, it's
    our education, but it seems so . . .
one-sided! Maybe in Sixth-Grade, things will work
    the other way around, so that sons
                  murder their fathers,
                  babies eat grownups,
and Snow White poisons
    her wicked step-mother. So far that's
the best reason to leave Fifth-Grade behind us.
    Still, we don't see why Science—at least
                  Dinny Lee's version—
                  has to be so . . . so
animalistic.
    That may be how life is, but we'd like
to put in a word—two words—for Other Things
    we could learn at Park School, Duncan Chu

says that the right phrase
for what we mean is

human interest:
what we want to study at Park School
is how people have managed to *avoid*
behaving like animals, instead
of becoming them.
Is Science only
a history of death?
Maybe we'll find out in Sixth-Grade that
no Fate is worse than death after all,
and that life is going to be ours.
Dear Mrs Masters,
if these suggestions
make sense to you, please
let us (and Dinny Lee) know about
what courses we'll be taking next year along
the lines we have designated here,
and the kind of books
we should be reading
over the summer.
(signed) Respectfully, the Fifth-Grade Class:
Judy Abrams, Nancy Akers, Jean Sturges, David Halperin,
David Stashower, Jane McCullough,
Arthur Englander,
Anne Wiebe, Lois
Hexter, Jeunesse Ames,
David McConnehey, Duncan Chu
and today's guests, Mike Rahn & Clark Taft
visiting from the Fourth-Grade Class

from *The Antioch Review*

Magdalene— The Seven Devils

◇ ◇ ◇

Mary, called Magdalene, from whom seven devils had been cast out
—Luke 8:2

The first was that I was very busy.
The second—I was different from you: whatever happened to you could
    not happen to me, not like that.

The third—I worried.
The fourth—envy, disguised as compassion.
The fifth was that I refused to consider the quality of life of the aphid,
the aphid disgusted me. But I couldn't stop thinking about it.
The mosquito too—its face.   And the ant—its bifurcated body.

Ok   the first was that I was so busy.

The second that I might make the wrong choice,
because I had decided to take that plane that day,
that flight, before noon, so as to arrive early
    and, I shouldn't have wanted that.

The third was that if I walked past the certain place on the street
    the house would blow up.

The fourth was that I was made of guts and blood with a thin layer
    of skin lightly thrown over the whole thing.

The fifth was that the dead seemed more alive to me than the living

The sixth—if I touched my right arm I had to touch my left arm, and if I touched the left arm a little harder than I'd first touched the right then I had to retouch the left and then touch the right again so it would be even.

The seventh—I knew I was breathing the expelled breath of everything that was alive and I couldn't stand it,

I wanted a sieve, a mask, a, I hate this word—cheesecloth— to breathe through that would trap it—whatever was inside everyone else that entered me when I breathed in

No. That was the first one.

The second was that I was so busy. I had no time. How had this happened? How had our lives gotten like this?

The third was that I couldn't eat food if I really saw it—distinct, separate from me in a bowl or on a plate.

Ok. The first was that I could never get to the end of the list.

The second was that the laundry was never finally done.

The third was that no one knew me, although they thought they did. And that if people thought of me as little as I thought of them then what was love?

The fourth was I didn't belong to anyone. I wouldn't allow myself to belong to anyone.

Historians would assume my sin was sexual.

The fifth was that I knew none of us could ever know what we didn't know.

The sixth was that I projected onto others what I myself was feeling.

The seventh was the way my mother looked when she was dying. The sound she made—the gurgling sound—so loud we had to speak louder to hear each other over it.

And that I couldn't stop hearing it—years later—
grocery shopping, crossing the street—

No, not the sound—it was her body's hunger
finally evident—what our mother had hidden all her life.

For months I dreamt of knucklebones and roots,
the slabs of sidewalk pushed up like crooked teeth by what grew underneath.

The underneath—that was the first devil.   It was always with me.
And that I didn't think you—if I told you—would understand any of this—

from *The American Poetry Review*

Memphis

◇　◇　◇

You like to pretend you will meet her again someday in Knoxville, Nashville,
　　Memphis.
Tennessee—state of forgiveness, of makeup sex, of uneaten ribs. O Memphis!

Drink more, hit on waitress with tattoo & pierced navel, slouch toward
　　gracelessness.
Imagine there are no consequences. What fails in your fantasies stays in Memphis.

Any home not your own offers a chance to shed skin & slither free from what is.
Ancient city covered with silt now, no earthen dam legible enough to protect
　　Memphis.

You are so prepared to be disappointed by Graceland that you fall in love with it.
How have I failed to mention the music? That is, after all, why you come to
　　Memphis.

Buy a shirt at B. B. King's, guzzle beer on Beale Street. Hell yeah, Elvis lives.
Just another plastic anagram. Why would anywhere be different? Why Memphis?

Sun sets over this river city: the transient slap & echo of blues. Water makes the
　　best witness.
If you never stand still, there's nowhere you can't end up. Why not Memphis?

None of us ever falls where we belong—we are ghosts on our way to someplace
　　else.
This is especially true in the American South. Write me a letter from Memphis.

If you think you are happy, you need a more accurate measure. Nothing lasts. Ask
     Ramses.
Floods will always find you, water seeking other water. Even here, even Memphis.

from *The Southern Review*

Aria

◇   ◇   ◇

1.

Tonight at a party we will say farewell
to a close friend's breasts, top surgery for months
she's saved for. Bundled close on a back step,
we wave a Bic lighter and burn her bra.
At first struggling to catch nylon aflame,
in awe we watch as all but the sheer black
underwire melts before forming a deep
quiet hole in the snow.
                        Sometimes the page
too goes quiet, a body that we've stopped
speaking with, a chest out of which music
will come if she's a drum flattened tight, if she's
pulled like canvas across a field, a frame
where curves don't show, exhalation without air.

Then this off-pitch soprano steals through.

2.

Then this off-pitch soprano steals through
a crack that's lit. A scarlet gap between
loose teeth. Interior trill. We're rustling open.
Out of a prohibited body why
long for melody? Just a thrust of air,
a little space with which to make this thistling
sound, stretch of atmosphere to piss through when

you're scared shitless. *Little sister, the sky*
is falling and I don't mind, I don't mind,
a line a girl, a prophet half my age,
told me to listen for one summer when
I was gutless, a big-mouthed carp that drank
down liters of algae, silt, fragile shale
while black-winged ospreys plummeted from above.

3.

While black-winged ospreys plummeted from above,
we were born beneath. You know what I mean?
I'll tell you what the girls who never love
us back taught me: The strain within will tune
the torqued pitch. In 1902 the last
castrato sang "Ave Maria."
His voice—a bifurcated swell. So pure
a lady screams with ecstasy. *Voce*
bianco! Breath control. Hold each note. Extend
the timbre. Pump the chest, that balloon room,
and lift pink lips, chin so soft and beardless,
a flutter, a flourish, a cry stretching beyond
its range, cruising through four octaves, a warbler,
a starling with supernatural restraint.

4.

A starling with supernatural restraint,
a tender glissando on a scratched LP,
his flute could speak catbird and hermit thrush.
It was the year a war occurred or troops
were sent while homicide statistics rose;
I stopped teaching to walkout, my arms linked
to my students to show a mayor who didn't
show. Seven hundred youth leaned on adults
who leaned back. We had lost another smart kid
to a bullet in the Fillmore, Sunnyside,
the Tenderloin. To love without resource

or peace. When words were noise, a jazz cut was steel.
I listened for Dolphy's pipes in the pitch dark:
A far cry. Epistrophy. A refusal.

5.

A far cry. Epistrophy. A refusal.
A nightingale is recorded in a field
where finally we meet to touch and sleep.
A nightingale attests
as bombers buzz and whir
overhead enroute to raid.
We meet undercover of brush and dust.
We meet to revise what we heard.
The year I can't tell you. The past restages
the future. Palindrome we can't resolve.
But the coded trill a fever ascending,
a Markov chain, discrete equation,
generative pulse, sweet arrest,
bronchial junction, harmonic jam.

6.

Bronchial junction, harmonic jam,
her disco dancing shatters laser light.
Her rock rap screamed through a plastic bullhorn
could save my life. Now trauma is a remix,
a beat played back, a circadian pulse we can't shake,
inherent in the meter we might speak,
so with accompaniment I choose to heal
at a show where every body that I press against
lip syncs: *I've got post binary gender chores . . .*
I've got to move. Oh, got to move. This box
is least insufferable when I can feel
your anger crystallize a few inches away,
see revolutions in your hips and fists.
I need a crown to have this dance interlude.

7.

I need a crown to have this dance interlude
or more than one. Heating flapjacks you re-
read "Danse Russe," where a man alone and naked
invents a ballet swinging his shirt around
his head. Today you're a dandier nude
in argyle socks and not lonely as you
slide down the hall echoing girly tunes
through a mop handle: *You make me feel like. . . .*
She-bop doo wop . . . an original butch
domestic. The landlord is looking through
the mini-blinds. Perched on a sycamore,
a yellow throated warbler measures your
schisms, fault lines, your taciturn vibrato.
Tonight, as one crowd, we will bridge this choir.

from *Beloit Poetry Journal*

So Where Are We?

◇   ◇   ◇

So where were we? The fiery
avalanche headed right at us—falling,

flailing bodies in mid-air—
the neighborhood under thick gray powder—

on every screen. I don't know
where you are, I don't know what

I'm going to do, I heard a man say;
the man who had spoken was myself.

What year? Which Southwest Asian war?
Smoke from infants' brains

on fire from the phosphorus hours
after they're killed, killers

reveling in the horror. The more obscene
the better it works. The point

at which a hundred thousand massacred
is only a detail. Asset and credit bubbles

about to burst. Too much consciousness
of too much at once, a tangle of tenses

and parallel thoughts, a series of feelings
overlapping a sudden sensation

felt and known, those chains of small facts
repeated endlessly, in the depths

of silent time. So where are we?
My ear turns, like an animal's. I listen.

Like it or not, a digital you is out there.
Half of that city's buildings aren't there.

Who was there when something was, and a witness
to it? The rich boy general conducts the Pakistani

heroin trade on a satellite phone from his cave.
On the top floor of the Federal Reserve

in an office looking out onto Liberty
at the South Tower's onetime space,

the Secretary of the Treasury concedes
they got killed in terms of perceptions.

Ten blocks away is the Church of the Transfiguration,
in the back is a Byzantine Madonna—

there is a God, a God who fits the drama
in a very particular sense. What you said—

the memory of a memory of a remembered
memory, the color of a memory, violet and black.

The lunar eclipse on the winter solstice,
the moon a red and black and copper hue.

The streets, the harbor, the light, the sky.
The blue and cloudless intense and blue morning sky.

from *Granta*

Tenor

◊   ◊   ◊

To break with the past
Or break it with the past
The enormous car-packed
Parking lot flashes like a frozen body
Of water a paparazzi sea
After take off

And because the pigeons laid eggs and could fly
Because the kittens could survive
Under the rubble wrapped
In shirts of the dead

And the half-empty school benches
Where each boy sits next
To his absence and holds him
In the space between two palms
Pressed to a face—
This world this hospice

from *Beloit Poetry Journal*

J O Y   K A T Z

Death Is Something Entirely Else

◇　◇　◇

Department of Trance
Department of Dream of Levitation
Department of White Fathom
Department of Winding
Sometimes my son orders me lie down
I like best when he orders me *lie down*　　　*close your eyes.*
Department of Paper Laid Gently
(Department of Sound of Sheets of Paper

　　　　　　　　　　　　　　　　he covers me with)
then sings
I like best the smallest sounds he makes then
Department of This Won't Sting
Am I slipping away
Department of Violet Static
as if he were a distant station?
Department of Satellite
My child says *you sleep*
Department of Infinitely Flexible Web
and covers my face with blankness
Department of Tap-Tapping the Vein
Department of Eyelash
I can't speak
　　　　　　　or even blink
　　　　　　　　　　　　　　or the page laid over my face will fall
Department of Clear Tape in Whorls and Double Helixes on the Wall
He says *mama don't look*
Department of You Won't Feel a Thing

NOELLE KOCOT

Poem

◊ ◊ ◊

With deepest reverence,
I shop for bones.

And what is the candy
And the daylight

And the horse without hunger?
Too many ducts for us to think of,

And here we are punishing the
Lines above our faces.

Enormity is a hoof
With unanswerable sounds,

And the void is filled with fire.
My dream is to fall apart,

To cry for a century,
But I have not cried, not at all.

I keep my distance like the tines
Of a fork from one another,

Dressing, undressing the fabulous wounds.
But now, back to our story,

It has coffee in it, a naked river.
Blessed are we who rapture

I cannot behold
Department of Pinprick
He will not behold
Department of Veils and Chimes
Lungs Afloat in Ether
I like this best
Department of Spider Vein
when I am most like dead
and being with him then, Department of Notes
Struck from Thin Glasses Successively at Random
I must explain to my child that sleep
                                        is not the same as dead
Department of Borderlessness
so that he may not be afraid of
Department of Fingertips Lightly on Eyelids
so I can lie and listen
not holding not carrying not working
Department of Becalmed   faint sound of him
                                        I am gone

His song is the door back to the room
I am composed of the notes

from *The Cincinnati Review*

How to Tie a Knot

◇ ◇ ◇

If I eat a diet of rain and nuts, walk to the P.O.
in a loincloth, file for divorce from the world of matter,
say *not–it!* to the sea oats, *not–it!* to the sky
above the disheveled palms, *not–it!* to the white or green oyster boats
and the men on the bridge with their fishing rods
that resemble so many giant whiskers,
if I repeat *this is not–it, this is not why I'm waiting here,*
will I fill the universe with all that is not-it
and allow myself to grow very still in the center of
this fishing town in winter? Will I look out past the cat
sleeping in the windowsill and say *not–it* garbage can,
not–it Long's Video Store, until I happen upon what
is not *not–it?* Will I wake up and *BEHOLD!*
the "actual," the "real," the "awe-thentic," the *IS?*
Instead I walk down to the Island Quicky, take a pound
of bait shrimp in an ice-filled baggy, then walk to the beach
to catch my dinner. Now waiting is the work
I'm waiting for. Now the sand crane dive-bombs the surf
of his own enlightenment because everything
is bait and lust and hard-up for supper.
            I came out here to pare things down,
wanted to be wind, simple as sand, to hear each note
in the infinite orchestra of waves fizzling out
beneath the rotting dock at five o'clock in the afternoon
when the voice that I call *I* is a one-man boat
slapping toward the shore of a waning illusion.
Hello, waves of salty and epiphanic distance. Good day,
bird who will eventually
go blind from slamming headfirst into the water.

What do you say, fat flounder out there
deep in your need, looking like sand speckled with
lying so still you're hardly there, lungs lifting
with such small air, flesh both succulent and flakey
when baked with white wine, lemon and salt, your
rolling toward their one want when the line jerks, a
clicks, and the rod bends, and you give up
the ocean floor for a mouthful of land.

from *The Cincinnati Review*

An electric wire, blessed be
The falling things about our faces,

Blessed is the socket of an eye
That lights the body, because

In the end, in the very end, it's
Just you. You and you. And you.

from *New American Writing*

MAXINE KUMIN

Either Or

◊   ◊   ◊

Death, in the orderly procession
of random events on this gradually
expiring planet crooked in a negligible

arm of a minor galaxy adrift among
millions of others bursting apart in
the amnion of space, *will,* said Socrates,

be either a dreamless slumber without end
or a migration of the soul from one place
to another, like the shadow of smoke rising

from the backroom woodstove that climbs
the trunk of the ash tree outside
my window and now that the sun is up

down come two red squirrels and a nuthatch.
Later we are promised snow.
So much for death today and long ago.

from *Ploughshares*

SARAH LINDSAY

Hollow Boom Soft Chime: The Thai Elephant Orchestra

◊　◊　◊

A sound of far-off thunder from instruments
ten feet away: drums, a log,
a gong of salvage metal. Chimes
of little Issan bells, pipes in a row, sometimes
a querulous harmonica.
Inside the elephant orchestra's audience,
bubbles form, of shame and joy, and burst.
Did elephants look so sad and wise,
a tourist thinks, her camera cold in her pocket,
before we came to say they look sad and wise?
Did mastodons have merry, unwrinkled faces?
Hollow boom soft chime, stamp of a padded foot,
tingle of renaat, rattle of angklung.
This music pauses sometimes, but does not end.

Prathida gently strokes the bells with a mallet.
Poong and his mahout regard the gong.
Paitoon sways before two drums,
bumping them, keeping time with her switching tail.
Sales of recordings help pay for their thin enclosure
of trampled grass. They have never lived free.
Beside a dry African river
their wild brother lies, a punctured balloon,
torn nerves trailing from the stumps of his tusks.
Hollow boom soft chime, scuff of a broad foot,

sometimes, rarely, a blatting elephant voice.
They seldom attend the instruments
without being led to them, but, once they've begun,
often refuse to stop playing.

from *Poetry*

The Autobiography of Khwaja Mustasim

◊   ◊   ◊

I stood for twenty years a chess piece in Córdoba, the black rook.
I was a parrot fed melon seeds by the eleventh caliph.
I sparked to life in a Damascus forge, no bigger than my own pupil.
I was the mosquito whose malarial kiss conquered Alexander.
I bound books in Bukhara, burned them in Balkh.
In my four hundred and sixteenth year I came to Qom.
I tasted Paradise early as an ant in the sugar bin of Mehmet Pasha's chief chef.
I was a Hindu slave stonemason who built the Blue Mosque without believing.
I rode as a louse under Burton's turban when he sneaked into Mecca.
I butchered halal in Jalalabad.
I had been a vulture just ten years when I looked down and saw Karbala set for
    me like a table.
I walked that lush Hafiz home and held his head while he puked.
I was one of those four palm trees smart-bomb-shaken behind the reporter's
    khaki vest.
I threw out the English-language newspaper that went on to hide the roadside
    bomb.
The nails in which were taken from my brother's coffin.
My sister's widowing sighed sand in a thousand Kalashnikovs.
I buzzed by a tube light, and three intelligence officers, magazines rolled,
    hunted me in vain.
Here I am at last, born in a city whose name, on General Elphinstone's 1842
    map, was misspelt "Heart."
A mullah for a mauled age, a Muslim whose memory goes back farther than
    the Balfour Declaration.

You may remember me as the grandfather who guided the gaze of a six-year-old Omar Khayyám to the constellations.
Also maybe as the inmate of a Cairo jail who took the top bunk and shouted down at Sayyid Qutb to please please please shut up.

from *The New Yorker*

Mrs. Mason and the Poets

◇　◇　◇

At that point I had lived with Mr. Tighe
so many years apart from matrimony
we quite forgot the world would call it sin.
We were, in letters of our friends at Pisa,
Mr. and Mrs. Mason, the common name
domesticating the arrangement. (Our friends
were younger, thinking it a novelty.)

You've heard about Lord Byron and his zoo,
how he befriended geese he meant to eat
and how they ruled his villa like a byre
with peacocks, horses, monkeys, cats and crows.
And our friend Shelley whom we thought so ill,
whose brilliant wife was palely loitering,
waiting to give birth and dreading signs
that some disaster surely must befall them.
Shelley of the godless vegetable love,
pursuer of expensive causes, sprite.
He had confided in me more than once
how his enthusiasms caused him pain
and caused no end of pain to those he loved.

Some nights I see his blue eyes thrashing back
and comprehend how grieved he was, how aged.
Genius, yes, but often idiotic.
It took too many deaths, too many drownings,
fevers, accusations, to make him see
the ordinary life was not all bad.

I saw him last, not at the stormy pier
but in a dream. He came by candlelight,
one hand inside a pocket, and I said,
You look ill, you are tired, sit down and eat.

He answered, *No. I shall never eat more.*
I have not a soldo left in all the world.

Nonsense, this is no inn—you need not pay.

Perhaps it is the worse for that, he said.
He drew the hand out of his pocket, holding
a book of poems as if to buy his supper.
To see such brightness fallen broke my heart,
and then, of course, I learned that he had drowned.

Once, they say, he spread a paper out
upon a table, dipped his quill and made
a single dot of ink. *That,* he said,
is all of human knowledge, and the white
is all experience we dream of touching.
If I should spread more paper here, if all
the paper made by man were lying here,
that whiteness would be like experience,
but still our knowledge would be that one dot.

I've watched so many of the young die young.
As evening falls, I know that Mr. Tighe
will come back from his stroll, and he will say
to humour me, *Why Mrs. Mason, how*
might you have spent these several lovely hours?

And I shall notice how a slight peach flush
illuminates his whiskers as the sun
rounds the palms and enters at our windows.
And I shall say, *As you have, Mr. Mason,*
thinking of lost friends, wishing they were here.

And he: *Lost friends? Then I should pour the wine.*

And I? What shall I say to this kind man
but *Yes, my darling, time to pour the wine.*

from *The Hudson Review* and *Umbrella*

Becca

◇   ◇   ◇

She says, *It's my birthday, I'm going tomorrow,*
What's your favorite font? What should I
have him write? Serifs, I say. *I like serifs.*
I like old typewriters, the keys little platters.
I don't answer the question about what to write.
The vellum of her back. I am not her mother,
who later weeps at the words written between
her shoulders. I get ready to retract the idea of serifs,
the pennants that pull the eye from one word
forward, but the eye loves a serif. When we
handwrite, we stop to add them to *I. Read this*
word like typeface, make me always published,
I am always a text. Write this on your back,
I want to say. Write that you are a lyric
and flying—serifed, syntactical. Becca chooses
Make of my life a few wild stanzas. She lies
on the bed while the artist marks her back,
his needle the harrow for her sentence. Make of
my life a place to stand, stopping-places, a series
of rooms, stances, *stare, stantia, stay.* She has
shown him a bird she wants perched above the final
word, *stanza.* It is a barn swallow—ink blue flash.
He says, toward the end, so she can know it will hurt
to ink so much blue, *I am filling in the stanza now,*
and he stings her right shoulder again and again,
filling the room of the bird. Make of my life
a poem, she asks me and him and her mother
as she walks away, make of my life something
wild, she says. I watch her strike out across

Number 10 Pond, the tattoo flashing with each stroke
and there is barely enough time to read it.

from *The American Poetry Review*

HONOR MOORE

Song

◇ ◇ ◇

Of sheets and skin and fur of him,
bed of ground and river, of land,
or tongue, of arms, the wanton field,
of flame and flowers, stalk of him,
harp, arboreal, steep and rush.
House him in the coil of my hair,
silk of him and open sea, flood, star,
toes of him, stickiness, of flesh.
Rind of him, gaze, of salt and heat,
face, food and blade, island in bright
bloom, bristle, blossom, all this night
lie long with him as dark flies fleet.
Transparent, filled up, emptied out,
here of him, here I find his mouth.

from *The Common*

MICHAEL MORSE

Void and Compensation (Facebook)

◊   ◊   ◊

My friends who were and aren't dead
are coming back to say hello.

There's a wall that they write things on.
They have status updates. *What are you doing right now?*

For the most part, they seem successful.
They have children, which I can only imagine.

The hairy kid we called *Aper,* I haven't heard
from him and wonder if in every contact

there are apologies inherent
for feelings hurt and falling out of touch—

I'm sorry in the way that dogs out back
bark at the nothing they're trying to name.

Now the missing turn up online,
the immanent unheard becoming memory.

We have conversations that are flat
or we speak to one another in threads,

a wall more kind than faces posted downtown
when tower dust settled and sky went blue again.

When Leo died we couldn't believe he wasn't hiding,
that his laugh would not sound out, announce his return.

What a laugh. Goofy. His. Purely his
and out loud like a dog barking at stars.

Something heavenly. An application
against insults or things that spill.

That was Leo. And he left.
I don't think he meant to go

before he found some beloved and made
someone in and not of his image.

I want to find Leo on Facebook.
I want to discover that he's a chemist

and tell him it's like high school all over
with so much living, it was nice, to be done

and to see and hear from you after so long.
You seem great. You look exactly the same.

from *Ploughshares*

Hate Mail

◇　◇　◇

You are a whore. You are an old whore.
Everyone hates you. God hates you.
He pretty much has had it with all women

But, let me tell you, especially you. You like
To think that you can think faster than
The rest of us—hah! We drive the car

In which you're a crash dummy! So
Why do you defy our Executive Committee
Which will never cede its floor to you? If a pig

Flew out of a tree & rose to become
A blimp—you would write a poem
About it, ignoring the Greater Good,

The hard facts of gravity. You deserve to be
Flattened by the Greater Good—pigs don't
Fly, yet your arrogance is that of a blimp

Which has long forgotten its place on this earth.
Big arrogance unmoored from its launchpad
Floating free, up with mangy Canadian honkers,

Up with the spy satellites and the ruined
Ozone layer which is, btw, caused by your breath,
Because you were born to ruin everything, hacking

Into the inspiration of the normal human ego.
You are not Queen Tut, honey, you are not
Even a peasant barmaid, you are an aristocrat

Of Trash, land mine of exploding rhinestones,
Crown of thorns, cabal of screech bats!
I am telling you this as an old friend,

Who is offering advice for your own good—
Change now or we will have to Take Measures—
If you know what I mean, which you do—

& now let's hear one of your fucked-up poems:
Let's hear you refute this truth any way you can.

from *Boston Review*

Daffodil

◇ ◇ ◇

A poet could not but be gay
—William Wordsworth

Don't you know, sweetheart,
less is more?

Giving yourself away
so quickly

with your eager trumpet—
April's rentboy

in your flock of clones,
unreasonably cheerful, cellulose,

as yellow as a crow's foot—*please.*
I don't get you.

Maybe it's me,
always loving what I can't have,

the bulb refusing itself,
perennial challenge.

I'd rather have mulch
than three blithe sepals from you.

I've never learned
how to handle kindness

from strangers.
It's uncomfortable, uncalled-for.

I'm into piss and vinegar,
brazen disregard,

the minimum-wage indifference
of bark, prickly pear.

Flirtation's tension:
I dare, don't dare.

But what would you know
about restraint,

binge-drinking
your way through spring,

botany's twink bucked
by lycorine, lethal self-esteem?

You who come and go
with the seasons,

bridge and tunnel.
You're all milk and no cow—

intimacy for beginners.
The blond-eyed boy stumbling home.

If I were you, I'd pipe down.
Believe me,

I've bloomed like you before.

from *Lambda Literary Review*

MARY OLIVER

In Provincetown, and Ohio, and Alabama

◊   ◊   ◊

Death taps his black wand and something vanishes. Summer, winter;
the thickest branch of an oak tree for which I have a special love; three
just hatched geese. Many trees and thickets of catbrier as bulldozers
widen the bicycle path. The violets down by the old creek, the flow
itself now raveling forward through an underground tunnel.

Lambs that, only recently, were gamboling in the field. An old mule,
in Alabama, that could take no more of anything. And then, what fol-
lows? Then spring again, summer, and the season of harvest. More
catbrier, almost instantly rising. (No violets, ever, or song of the old
creek.) More lambs and new green grass in the field, for their happi-
ness *until.* And some kind of yellow flower whose name I don't know
(but what does that matter?) rising around and out of the half-buried,
half-vulture-eaten, harness-galled, open-mouthed (its teeth long and
blackened), breathless, holy mule.

from *Five Points*

Where Do We Go After We Die

◇   ◇   ◇

They're at their old favorite bar. The funeral's over. The question
Commands and divides them. One sees the pictograph
Of the great wheel; another, a figure of closed eyes,
Another, the heavenly throne surrounded by a choir of angels,
Remembered from Sunday School. Scripture,
From many sources, is cited, science invoked
And contradictions exposed. The peacemaker
Among them declares that all the stories are true
But on different planes, you can travel among them
When you're dead, if you want to, even this one,
And find those you cared for and follow them around,
Walk through their pratfalls and the wreckage
And be amazed again at the poignant bravery of the living,
Then the fabulist adds that you want to help, but you can't,
You're a ghost, that's a rule in all the stories,
And that's why both compassion and a coolness of spirit
Can be felt on every street, making the best of a bad deal.
Someone tells a story about Jon, who died
And gathered them here. It brings them to tears.
Another story, and they curse his transgressions.
Then other friends who have died, story and commentary
And rebuttal, they drink, they complicate,
They begin to forget the quirks they loved
And the spirit that flows like a river powerful enough
To ignore the seasons. The lights flash off and on,
The bartender is drying the last of the glasses,

Stories slide under the chairs into the shadows,
Speech reverts to its ancient, parabolic self—*Yea,*
Though I walk through the valley—
And actions lose their agency—*It came to pass*—
The things of the world become scarce,
And what's left spreads its wings
And flies around among them, like bats at dusk.

from *New Ohio Review*

ALICIA OSTRIKER

Song

◇   ◇   ◇

Some claim the origin of song
was a war cry
some say it was a rhyme
telling the farmers when to plant and reap
don't they know the first song was a lullaby
pulled from a mother's sleep
said the old woman

A significant
factor generating my delight in being
alive this springtime
is the birdsong
that like a sweeping mesh has captured me
like diamond rain I can't
hear it enough said the tulip

lifetime after lifetime
we surged up the hill
I and my dear brothers
thirsty for blood
uttering
our beautiful songs
said the dog

from *Poetry*

ERIC PANKEY

Sober Then Drunk Again

◊   ◊   ◊

On the lightning-struck pin oak,
On the swayed spine of the Blue Ridge,
                                        a little gold leaf.

Once I drank with a vengeance.
Now I drink in surrender.
The thaw cannot keep me from wintering in.

I prepare for death when I should prepare
For tomorrow and the day after
                            and the day after that.

A clinker of grief where once hung my heart.

Memory—moon-drawn, tidal.
The moon's celadon glaze dulls in the morning's cold kiln.

from *The Cincinnati Review*

Samara

◊　◊　◊

1.

At first they're yellow butterflies
whirling outside the window—

but no: they're flying seeds.
An offering from the maple tree,

hard to believe the earth-engine capable of such invention,
that the process of mutation and dispersal
will not only formulate the right equations

but that when they finally arrive they'll be so
. . . *giddy?*

2.

Somewhere Darwin speculates that happiness
should be the outcome of his theory—

those who take pleasure
will produce offspring who'll take pleasure,

though he concedes the advantage of the animal who keeps death in mind
and so is vigilant.

And doesn't vigilance call for
at least an ounce of expectation,
imagining the lion's tooth inside your neck already,

for you to have your best chance of outrunning the lion

on the arrival of the lion.

3.

When it comes time to "dedicate the merit"
my Buddhist friends chant *from the ocean of samsara*
may I free all beings—

at first I misremembered, and thought
the word for the seed the same.

Meaning "the wheel of birth and misery and death,"
nothing in between the birth and death but misery,

surely an overzealous bit of whittlework
on the part of *Webster's Third New International Unabridged*

(though if you eliminate dogs and pie and swimming
feels about right to me—

oh shut up, Lucia. The rule is: you can't nullify the world
in the middle of your singing.)

4.

In the Autonomous Vehicle Laboratory
Roboseed is flying.
It is not a sorrow though its motor makes an annoying sound.

The doctoral students have calculated

the correct thrust-to-weight ratio and heave dynamics.
On YouTube you can watch it flying in the moonlight
outside the engineering building with the fake Ionic columns.

I said "sorrow" for the fear that in the future all the beauties
will be replaced by replicas that have more glare and blare and bling.
Roboseed, roborose, roboheart, robosoul—

this way there'll be no blight
on any of the cherished encapsulations

when the blight was what we loved.

5.

They grow in chains from the Bigleaf Maple, chains
that lengthen until they break.
In June,

when the days are long and the sky is full
and the swept pile thickens
with the ones grown brown and brittle,

oh see how I've underestimated the persistence
of the lace in their one wing.

6.

Is there no slim chance I will feel it

when some molecule of me
(annealed by fire, like coal or glass)

is drawn up in the phloem of a maple
(please scatter my ashes under a maple)

so my speck can blip out
on a stem sprouting out of the fork of a branch,

the afterthought of a flower
that was the afterthought of a bud,

transformed now into a seed with a wing,
like the one I wore on the tip of my nose

back when I was green.

from *The American Poetry Review*

Improvisation on Yiddish

◇　◇　◇

I've got you in my pocket, Ich hob mir fer pacht.
It sees me and I cannot spell it.

Ich hob dich in bud, which means I see you as if
You were in the bathtub naked: I know you completely.

Kischkas: guts. Tongue of the guts, tongue
Of the heart naked, the guts of the tongue.

Bubbeh loschen. Tongue of my grandmother
That I can't spell in these characters I know.

I know "Hob dich in bud" which means I see you
And through you, tongue of irony. Intimate.

Tongue of the dear and the dead, tongue of death.
Tongue of laughing in the guts, naked and completely.

Bubbeh loschen, lost tongue of the lost, "Get away
From me" which means, *come closer*: Gei

Avek fun mir, Ich hob dich in bud. I see you
Completely. Naked. I've got you in my pocket.

from *The Threepenny Review*

DEAN RADER

Self-Portrait
as Dido to Aeneas

◇   ◇   ◇

We wake: the night star-scorched & stained, morning fetal and uncoiling:
everything lifting: treehush and moondive: you at the window, the window

at day's limn. The day (heart's fulcrum) lists. Hear me: even if the bed
is an iron net, and the mattress a cage of twine and sawgrass: even if my legs

are bars and my arms are bars, the body's chain of sweat and skin
is no prison: it's the floating cell of the ship that will lock you down.

from *The Cincinnati Review*

The Road to Emmaus

◊ ◊ ◊

for Nathan Gebert

I.

The chair from Goodwill smelled of mildew.
I sat with Sister Ann, a Franciscan.
In her small office, at the Cenacle Retreat House,
right off Dixie Highway in Lantana, Florida,
I began my story—
it was an interview, much of life is an interview.
She said I did not need to pay her, but donations,
yes, donations were appreciated:
they could be left anonymously in a plain white envelope
that she could take back to the cloister.
She was dressed in a turtleneck and a denim jumper.
She could have been mistaken in a grocery store for an aging housewife.
My meetings with her went on for a few years.

I had come to speak about Durell.
I did not know how to end sentences about Durell.
He had taught me—what? To live? Not to wince in the mirror?
What? There were so many ways to end my sentence.
He was an unlikely candidate for so many things.
Outside, it was always some subtle variation of summer.
I paused, then spoke urgently, not wanting to forget some fact,
but much I knew I would forget or remember in a way my own,

which would not exactly be correct, no, not exactly.
Durell was dead, I said, and I needed to make sense of things.

Sister Ann's face was open, fragile—
parts were chipped as on a recovered fresco.
Above her gray head,
a garish postcard of the Emmaus scene,
the colors off, as if painted by numbers, with no concern for shading—
the style of it had an unoriginal Catholic institutional uniformity.
There it hung, askew in its golden drugstore frame.
It was the scene from the end of Luke, the two disciples,
one named Cleopas, the other anonymous,
forever mumbling Christ's name, and with them,
the resurrected Christ masquerading as a stranger.
They were on their way to that town, Emmaus,
seven miles out from Jerusalem,
gossiping about the impress of Christ's vanishing—
they argued about whether to believe what they had seen;
they were restless, back and forth the debate went—
when there is estrangement there is little peace.

II.

Every time we met, Sister Ann prayed first.
At times, my recollections blurred or a presumption would reverse.
Sister Ann told me Durell was with me *still,*
in a more intimate way than when he lived.
She frequently lost her equilibrium, as older people sometimes do,
before settling into her worn-out chair
where she listened to me, week after week.

The day I met Durell, I said, the morning light was clear,
startling the town with ornament.
The steeple of Christ Church held the horizon in place,
or so I imagined, as if it had been painted first
with confident amounts of titanium white
before the rest was added. Trees clattered.
The reiterating brick puzzle of Cambridge brightened—

Mass Avenue, Mount Auburn, Dunster, Holyoke—
proclaimed a new September, and new students trudged the streets.
Every blood-warm structure was defined in relief.

Hours before, while the moon's neck wobbled on the Charles
like a giraffe's, or the ghost of a giraffe's neck,
I imagined Durell labored, having slept only a few hours,
caged in his worries of doctor bills, no money,
and running out of people to ask for it:
mulling over mistakes, broken love affairs—
a hospital orderly, a man upstairs,
he probably mumbled unkind epithets about blacks and Jews,
even though the men he loved *were* blacks and Jews.
Some of his blasphemies, if you want to call them that,
embarrassed me in front of Sister Ann,
but she seemed unflappably tolerant.

At sixty, he was unemployable.
He had taught school and guarded buildings,
each job ending worse than the last.
His refrain was always: "It is not easy being an impoverished aristocrat."
He spoke with the old Harvard accent,
I can *still* hear it, I will probably *always* hear it,
with New York City, the North Shore and the army mixed in,
the *a*'s broadened, the *r*'s were flat, the *t*'s snapped—
so a sentence would calibrate to a confident close,
like "My dee-ah boy, *that* is *that.*"
He lived on 19 Garden Street in a rent-controlled studio
on the second floor, number 25; he said the "25" reminded him of Christmas.

At eleven o'clock,
he probably pulled on his support hose,
increasing the circulation in his legs, blotched green and black.
Next, he would have locked the door with his gold key
and moved deliberately, his smile beleaguered.
Bowing to Miss Littlefield in the landlord's office
at the building's dark cubbyhole of an entrance:
they probably spoke of Queen Elizabeth II,
her disappointments, for Miss Littlefield and he were Royalists both.

Then Durell began to move towards me, entering the Square.
Breathing heavily, he might have passed the Brattle
advertising *Judgment at Nuremberg*—
inside the shut black theatrical box where the world repeated the past,
Maximilian Schell interrogated Judy Garland and Montgomery Clift;
Marlene Dietrich let the phone ring and ring.
Maybe he passed the Store 24 sign, bright orange,
passed Nini's Corner where sex magazines were stacked like a cliff.
Maybe, maybe. But, maybe not.
Maybe he went another way.

Then I recalled how the T shook that place,
the subway grates pushing up the scent of rat-life and all things fallen,
mixing with Leavitt & Peirce exuding its masculine snuff.
Down Plympton Street he might have gone, past the Grolier,
which I always remembered, for some reason, as closed,
gilded with spines of poetry books for its reredos.
Yes, he probably, most likely, certainly, did that.
Sister Ann wondered if I thought he paused.
I thought not—
poetry offered him no solutions.

At twelve o'clock,
the chairperson called our AA meeting to order.
We called ourselves "The Loony Nooners,"
and met in a Lutheran church basement.
We ate salads out of Tupperware,
shaking the contents like dice to mix the dressing.
Some knitted. Schizophrenics lit multiple cigarettes.
Acne-pocked Kate wanted to be a model,
Electroshock Mike read paperbacks,
and an Irish professor named Tom
welcomed Tellus, who could not get over Nam.
Darkened figures in the poor light, we looked like the burghers of Calais,
and smelled of brewed coffee, smoke, perfume, urine, human brine.
We were aristocrats of time:
"I have twenty-one years," "I have one week," "I have one day."
I have often thought we were like first-century Christians—
a strident, hidden throng, electrified by a message.

Or, another way of thinking of us
is that we were inconvenient obstacles
momentarily removed, much to the city's relief.
From each window well, high heels and business shoes hurried.
Durell H., as he was known to us, took his place,
his thick hair fixed as the waves of an 1800s nautical painting
(perhaps he kept it set with hair spray?),
his Tiffany ring polished to a brilliance,
he set himself apart in his metal folding chair.
He had the clotted girth of Hermann Göring.
What was he thinking about?
Was he thinking about blood clots and possible aneurysms?
Imperious, behind prism-like trifocals,
quietly he said to me, "I've grown as fat as Elizabeth Taylor."

III.

The meeting ended and Durell folded his metal chair.
He hated his Christian name—
"Durell," he said, "Who names their child Durell?"
Moving among the crowd, listening to success and failure,
he passed out meeting lists, literature, leaflets.
Durell sponsored men, he referred to them as "pigeons."
I met him that day. I was his last.

After that, every day we spoke on rotary phones.
I was young and spoke as if my story was the only one.
I told him I had underlined key passages in Plato's *Symposium*,
told him I had been graded unfairly on Dante's *Inferno* and *Purgatorio*,
told him my schedule might not allow for the *Paradiso*.
He matched my telling with listening, advising,
and more listening, mostly over the phone,
and the more he listened the more he was alone.
"Why was that?" Sister Ann asked.
It was some sort of offering, perhaps.
At times it seemed he needed to guarantee a pardon,
that old Catholic idea of indulgences
lurked somewhere there unspoken,
as if he believed a larger offering might guarantee a larger pardon.

Such a task demanded his increased singleness.
Yes, that was true. Or was it?
I had trouble settling on the right words with Sister Ann.
Many of my words were not exactly right, the syntax awkward.
I kept having trouble translating Durell, so much I guessed.
How to know?
(Why hadn't I asked him more questions?
He wasn't the sort that invited questions, I *do* remember that.)
Another way of saying it was that when he was with me,
on the phone, then and only then, did he seem to move in truth
and in his truths, reprimanding and hard,
he was made more singular. Maybe that was it.
Whatever the case, he listened, he listened to me.
I missed his listening.
Listening, Sister Ann said, is a memorable form of love.

After the meeting, he gave me his calling card.
The cards were placed inside his compulsively polished silver card case,
the black capitals raised on their ecru background,
containing his name, bracketed by a "Mr." and a "Jr."—
the "Mr." denoting lost civility,
the "Jr." tallying a lineage that did not bridge.
As we walked down Church Street, the bells of St. John the Evangelist rang.
The road was bright, the road full.
Behind the brown gate with the thick black rusted latch,
the monks sang, "It is well, it is well, with my soul, with my soul."
We peered in at bookshop clerks locating titles,
watch repairmen bent over lit ocular devices, fixing movements,
florists, hands wet, arranging stems and branches broken.
We saw ourselves reflected.
I laughed with deference, the way a student laughs before a teacher.
His skin was flecked with milk-blues, lead-whites, earthen reds.
In dress and demeanor he was as rigid as a toy soldier,
for he was a part of a republic with standards, atrophied, devoted to order.

Everyone found him impossible,
including, at times, me.
Of queers, his word for what he was but could not admit to,
he said, "You know in the army they could never be trusted."
I mentioned romantic love.

In profile, a silhouette, he paused.
He said, "It has been very vexing, indeed."
By his tone, I knew never to ask again.
A decorum of opprobrium kept him whole,
and so he guarded himself with intensity.
Maybe, Sister Ann suggested, he was guarding me.

Durell said, "I've whittled my world down to no one,
Spencer, with the possible exception of you."

IV.

"What happened then?" Sister Ann asked.
He excused himself with a handshake, his palms soft as bread dough
from all the Jergens he had slathered on,
and then he probably returned to his ambry of a studio,
a place where I would be one of his only visitors.
Although he handed out his number, he did not always answer.
I remember . . . (What do I remember?) . . .
I was free to turn away but the moment I looked back,
Durell would come back to me,
waiting for me. It seems to me now, after all this time,
few things have as much fidelity as the past.

I remember he had nailed memorabilia above his head
as one would place stones to fortify a castle:
a photograph of him in the army, liberating people, undoing Russian codes;
a framed marriage license from England
(although the marriage failed, he often mumbled her name);
his framed diploma, Harvard, and over the corner hung
his graduation cap's faded black tassel.
Next to his pill bottles, an Edward VIII coronation mug he doted on,
commemorating an event that never took place.
Maybe he made a bread and baloney sandwich.
Maybe he stepped over the rolled-up tag-sale carpet and drew the shades.
By late evening, he might have jotted down notes about God,
obedient as he was to the twelve steps of AA.
He might have written in his tightly looped feminine penmanship,
informed by the Palmer Method,

and later repeated a phrase or two to me over the phone.
Or maybe he read from his *Twenty-Four Hours a Day* book
to find a rule maybe, or to search for a sanctuary.
Or maybe he listened to the Reverend Peter Gomes on the radio,
The Plummer Professor of Christian Morals at Harvard,
for he often mentioned how he loved the preacher's parallel constructions,
yes, maybe he did that, maybe, possibly, he did that.

And then, perhaps, he slept a bit
before the whole routine began once more
with the support hose, the hair spray, Miss Littlefield, the sex magazines,
the Grolier, the folding chair, the meeting, the calling card.
How crazy America was, he said, how he wanted to leave,
but he never left town, except jolting trips to the hospital
in an ambulance down all those brick roads.

V.

I lived in Cambridge two years.
After that, wherever I moved, we spoke, daily, over the phone, on land-
       lines—
talking and listening, listening and talking, for *fifteen* years:
"You alright?" "Yes. You?"
In all that time, I saw him only once more, and by then he was nearly blind.
In all that time, we barely touched one another.
Why our relationship required its rood screen,
I could not fully explain to Sister Ann,
indeed, I can never seem to properly explain it to anyone.
But I have tried, and I will probably always keep trying.
But if I get nothing right,
I must try to get a nuance of our friendship
and his sponsorship right—
we were bound, bound by a vow, a vow of attention
(there are many causes for attention, among them redemption).
Our attention concerned the spirit,
although that sounds pious and we were not so pious,
we were more selfish, more human than pious.
What else can I say?
I needed a liberator

and liberators can come in some unexpected guises.
I may never wholly explain the two of us.
Perhaps the spirit defies the human mind,
even after all my time with Sister Ann.

Finally, from a hospital, came the report of Durell's last day.
A charge nurse said: "I touched the gangrene leg, pink flesh was coming back."
His compliments had increased the more his life failed.
In the final week, he quoted Cole Porter songs to me—
You're a Bendel bonnet, a Shakespeare sonnet, you're Mickey Mouse . . .
I did not repeat the rhymes to Sister Ann.
Who Durell was and why he did what he did and why he hid
what he hid I kept asking her.
Sister Ann quoted from Deuteronomy:
"I set before you life and death . . . choose life."

Old pigeon flying back,
when I arrived at the hospital his body was gone.
The formalities were few,
for he had become a ward of the state.
The staff gave me a brown grocery bag of his things:
a roll of dimes, a pair of shoes, a belt buckle, an Einstein quote,
something about mediocre minds.
Afterwards, I went through Cambridge and found the meeting gone.
Night was coming.
Blindness worked on the people, shops, churches, streets.
No one knew me.
People said: "Where will we go?" and "What will we eat?"
I thought I recognized this or that face, but no, no, too much time had passed.
On Church Street, restaurants had replaced bookstores.
Windows on Mass Avenue shone with chandeliers.
Someone backed up photographing with a flash.
"Hold still," they said, "hold still."
A new set of homeless people pleaded,
coins rattled inside the used coffee cups they shook.
Everyone moved with packages, briefcases, textbooks, flash cards, cell phones,
        flowers.
The Charles advanced, determined as a hearse,
its dark waters gathering up every unattached thing.

An umber, granular dusk-light fell on the elms over Harvard Yard as they
swayed dark and slow
like the chords in the waltz from Copland's *Rodeo*.
There I stood, unsure of which way to go.
The light had more ghosts in it as it must have had that day in Emmaus.

VI.

Suddenly, Sister Ann announced our last meeting.
Down the linoleum hallway,
Sister Katherine and Sister Ruth moved and prayed.
Their numbers had dropped from seven to six,
and the nuns decided the Retreat House would close.
Soon, the chapel and offices would be leveled and replaced with condominiums.
In the halls, the swoosh-snap of duct tape yanked, pulled and cut,
straps tightened, vans bleating, and backing up into the back,
weather reports exchanged with the movers.
Sister Ann told me about herself that final time:
parents dead, alcoholic brother dead,
the brother embarrassed she had been a nun.
She opened her Bible on the shipping box between us,
leaned in, her hearing aids on, her silver crucifix knocking on her chest.
Above her head, a nail where the Emmaus scene had hung.

I asked: "What caused him to remain?"
Why did he want freedom for me?
Sister Ann spoke then of the Gospel of John
and the Samaritan woman at the well,
the one married nearly as many times as Elizabeth Taylor,
and how when Christ listened to her she became the first evangelist.
It was Christ's longest conversation with anyone, Sister Ann said.
The Samaritan woman's life changed because Christ listened to her.

John K., from the meetings, dead now too, once said:
"Oh, I knew Durell. He was odd. But we're all odd you know."
All I know now
is the more he loved me the more I loved the world.

VII.

I lost track of Sister Ann.
I have often thought about her and all the time she spent with me.
I have wanted to tell her now for some time
that not long after the cloister closed, Durell's sister located me,
leaving a message on my answering machine,
(it was still the time of answering machines),
inviting me to her winter house in Boynton Beach.

Durell's sister gave me directions.
She was quite close to me, as it turned out.
She had some of Durell's belongings that she wanted me to have.
"There isn't much," she said.
"But still, I think you should have what's here."
Durell spoke of his sister often,
but I did not know his family.
However, when we met, we recognized each other
as one sometimes recognizes what one has never seen before.

I said to her: "He knew me better than anyone."
The sentence surprised us.
We sat by the pool in her gated country club.
The Florida evening was a watercolor in the making,
colors bleeding into striking mistakes.
After all the members withdrew,
she said, "There are many things you do not know about my brother."
A worker folded terry cloth towels under a bamboo hut.
Her voice halted as voices halt
when words have been withheld.
"They called him names," she said, "A nancy boy, a priss, a sissy, a fairy . . ."
The pool's tempos ceased
until the silence about us was the silence in a palace.

Light disappeared everywhere.
The sun fell. She looked away,
said that he'd been to the army language school,
learned German and Russian, played the organ in his spare time,
mentioned he'd taken music with Copland at Harvard
(he had received a "gentleman's 'C'"—

the "C" stood for Copland she said he *always* said—
which made us laugh and seemed to beckon him to us).
He had hoped for an army career, she went on,
and then she mumbled something about a little German town,
I think she said it was in Schleswig-Holstein, near Lübeck,
where he was stationed while borders were being redrawn,
the letters stopping, the army, the men, something, the drink . . .
and then her words fell and sank
into subtle variations of all that goes unsaid.

We heard the distant sound of a train on its track,
crossing the Florida map going brown then black.
He became difficult, isolated—
she spoke softly then like the penitent.
He was always asking for money.
As his requests persisted she began to screen her calls.
"It became easier to tell him I had not been home," she said.
His behavior was affecting her marriage.
She chose never to introduce her children to Durell.
Perhaps he had a mental illness, perhaps he invented—
perhaps, perhaps, perhaps—
but no, she pressed on, perhaps it *was* his sexuality, he was *too* sensitive . . .
"People can be cruel," she said.
She felt he had never adjusted to cruelty
as if cruelty was something that one needed to adjust to.
Later, he was picked up for charges of soliciting sex.
And the more she told me, the less I knew.
All about us, a stillness began to displace the light
and Durell was there, and no longer there, staining that stillness.
After an estrangement ends there comes a great stillness,
the greater the estrangement the greater the stillness.
Across the parking lot, a gate rattled.

I told her he often said his life had been a failure,
I tried to convince him otherwise, but he never believed me.
Half a century ago, she broke off contact.
Her protracted estrangement made her look ill.
"Please, please," she said.
Her voice trailed off,
although what she was pleading for was not clear.

No, no, she did not want her grandchildren to know.
Subtle variations of Florida evening light withdrew with finality.
The pool brightened with moonlight, the color of snow.
The pool was still.
Darkness spilled everywhere.
There we were,
a man and a woman sitting in cushioned lounge chairs,
as if the world would always be an endless pair of separated things.
We did not touch each other.
We were still a long time.

from *Poetry*

Wax

◊   ◊   ◊

Family portrait with French Revolution and cancer

Tussaud is said to have knelt herself at the cooling bath
to mold him: Marat, "just after he had been killed

by Charlotte Corday. He was still warm, and his bleeding body
and the cadaverous aspect of his features presented a picture
replete with horror."

        Now, the dripping head remains exactly

as it once looked, according to the placards, and to which
the famous painting can attest,

though what one says and what is history
are each rarely certain: here are only fragments

of what is left: the white sheet swaddling
the head, white body and bath, lank arm splayed
and the pallid face with its Egyptian cheekbones—

        In the painting,
death comes in the form of a slight slit
delicately emblazoned on the right

pectoral: how tiny must have been that organ
for such a small wound to finish him. Not

like this wax man's heart, which must be large,
dangerous, intractable, worse than yours as the knife's great size
and placement indicate. Death

is not a small thing here. It takes work
to make it exact. It takes diligence.

> *Look,* the doctors said,
> as they took us in the room. *The new cells with the old ones.*
> And they held the little chart up to the light.

*

Hands snatching in the plaster, the eye
sockets, lip cleft: all Tussaud could take back to reconstruct
cire perdue's inverse procedures: to coat the wax
on plaster instead, favor the viscous

over molten metals; Tussaud's uncle, Curtius, taught her,
taking out the little calipers and stylus, looking
at the body and only seeing it, stopping thought
in order to make it spectacle. "Curtius

has models of kings, great writers, beautiful women,"
noted Mercier. "One sees the royal family
seated at his artificial banquet—The crier calls from the door:

Come in, gentlemen, come see the grand banquet; come in, *c'est tout
comme à Versailles!*"

> Come and look. The king
> is seated by the emperor. He is just your size

though his clothes are finer, and now you see the long face
is less attractive than imagined, the crab-like hand curls
over plated fork and knife: you are so close, you can walk beside him,

pointing out the little similarities, the curved
and moistened lip, mild smile, fat pads
of the cheeks: all of it so close it hurts the eyes to pinpoint

just where the light is coming from, to give it shape,
distance by giving it a perspective altogether

different from yourself. *List all the family members*
with a history of this condition. Today,

*

on the first floor of Madame Tussaud's Wax Museum
you can find celebrities and sports stars, every politician of note
though you will not see these same figures five years in a row:

there is a death even for the deathless, objects
that depend on reputation to survive,

while the bodies in the chambered basement fever
in their blood-stained gowns. They can live forever

inside our terror, as in Florence, where once they sculpted
skeletoned ex-votos out of wax, oil-stained skins
appearing to stretch even as they stayed frozen, recalling Dante's belief
that the medium's malleability would retain whatever power

could be impressed upon it: a face, a ring, a life force.

It was a plague year. Churches
were filled with offerings: friezes of figures
writhing with disease, infants staked

in their parents' grips. The wax gives each body
illness' vivid texture, yellow skin, purple skin, skin that blackens
at the joints, all the colors corruption takes

as the bodies too collapse themselves to shelves
on shelves of flesh: the family become a single,

swarming mass of misery, as each ex-voto was itself
a prayer but altogether became a panic:
Take this shape, take this

body that is better than myself, that can be
burned down, melted, added to, can accrue
new filigree and detail: this one will survive
where the other won't. Look: the wax

shares our secrets of birth and age, but unlike us keeps renewal
stored inside the cells.
                                        The doctors
                took out their pens. They wrote down all the family
                members with this condition: grandmother, grandfather,
                aunt, uncle, father, mother, who

                was it among us who hadn't been touched? There
                the ring of candles smoking gold beside the casket.

                And so we looked and looked, the mother's
                father's face frozen in repose—

                You have to look, the doctors said. And turned

                                        *

the human into map, drew bodies that could be
chart and information traced through centuries of experiment.

How many bodies to make the one body, endow the corpse
with attributes of life?

To keep it mute, intemporal—

                                And so the medieval
manuscript's *écorchés* playing the lute, riding horses,
striding their bloodless legs into town. Here
one skeleton tilts a skull in his palm, his own bone face tilted toward us:

                Genius lives on

while all else is material scrolled atop the vellum in its little,
withering snicker: it is all material here: all

answer and answer for the doctors,
and when the manuscript wasn't enough they scraped
the hive's glass scales with a knife.

They pounded and shaped, they took skulls
and poured on paraffin for skin
to give the blank bone personality again.

The wax could go where the mind was stuck.
It abandoned the map.

                    *You're
        a visual person,* the doctors said. *Imagine this,*
        and pointed to a color, a stain, an opening.

        I'd needed more and so they gave me more. They made
        an anatomy of me.

                            *

In the museum, families want to take their pictures
with the murderers. They pace
the chamber's cavern to stare into black pockets
of shock, cave after cave:

it was Tussaud who thought to bring in the death,
though hadn't it always been here?

Here is the killer with his handsome face.
Here is Manson, Bundy, Hitler,
the Terror's row of heads still spiked on stakes:

you can see into the cavern

of the jaw, and what is that feeling
its way out through the neckhole, these dead

of the dead, these never-dead,
where to look disperses what we think we see
the second it enters us?

The world is all brain, and does it matter that the thing before us
is a replication?

Even the wax only holds its breath—

And here is pancreas and breast, ovary, uterus, veins

that spangle fragmentary ropes, a negative
of this view outside my window where snow
on the hills creeps downward, turns fall trees in their fog beauty
necrotic, ghost.

The code, simply, degenerates. On a table,

*

the head of Robespierre, Fouquier de Tinville.
They are here still, some personality crawls

like an animal into its tiny hole, fits itself there, invites us in,
then repels us: back, back: we are the kings here still and you

cannot join us, and when they marched the busts of the ministers
from Curtius's house ("They demanded," he wrote Tussaud, "insistently
the citizens"), the busts were burned, were violently attacked.

The real has no limits, and still, is full of limit.

We think the heart matters. We think the breath,

too, and they do, that is what the wax says, and then
denies it: you are a king, too, and if you have loved him so long
by his symbol, here is something more exact.

Otherwise, why keep a real

guillotine crouched in the corner, why real
period clothes, real blood-stained shoes, no glass
so that when you go to the bathroom later
you are surprised to see the face in the mirror

twist into its expressions?

And the long corridors opened, and the doctors moved their hands
across my mother's breasts, her hips, they marked on charts the places
that were familiar. We used to joke

about the pesticides her father used, little silver canister swinging
at his hip. You could hear how close he was
in the garden by that panicked clatter, the stupid
immigrant. The tomatoes were silver after he'd finished.

And the radiation after X's polio. And the pills
the doctors pushed for Y. And the chemicals with which they infused
our napkins, our pencils, our mattresses, our milk—

*

Look how the wax imbibes our novelty and richness.
It takes on some of our power as well, the blood paint
of the Christ statue seeming
to run, to swell. For centuries they argued

how to divide him, man or God, till Calenzuoli shaped
a wax man's head then split the face
to find it: scalp flayed over the intact portion of his crown, flesh halo

where the passive gray eyes flicker and the stripped muscles gleam.

What is man is all red and red, tendon, cartilage
glimmering with a sheen of beef fat,
while the rest is the expression

of a patience endured through pain: our image
of the image of Christ, the exactness
of his interiority, the wet formulations of the mind.

"Eye, nose, lip / the tricks
of his frown, his forehead; nay,
the pretty dimples of his chin and cheek—

Would you not deem it breath'd? And that those veins
did verily bear blood?"

*

                        I had noticed that they took
            certain patients' families into a room
            during the operations. Separated them
            from where the others waited,
            so it was obvious when the doctors came
            and led a group into the little room, and shut the door.

            You could hear the muffled something, the scuttle
            in the dark that signaled pain,

            which was why I began to sing, *It's fine,*
            during the operation, cheerful, witless, *It's fine, it's fine,*
            so long as they don't take us into that little room

            which is what they did, three hours later, the doctor
            and his trout-faced resident.
                                We have some news,
            the doctor said, and as the door shut my father
            turned to me with a look that read,
            I will never forgive you.

            So many models, so many bits of grotesquery—

In the museum is Robert-François Damiens who,
in 1757, was ordered to have his flesh ripped

with pincers and, by proclamation, "on those places poured
molten lead, boiling oil, resin, wax,
body quartered by horses, his limbs consumed by fire."

The portrait of this pain, in its own way, a kind of compliment.

To make this man's suffering significant because
prohibitive, because

it would be the most intense form of privacy imaginable.

122

They tortured a person

out of the body that they killed, and then they changed this:
Guillotin remodeling the blade to sculpt the new
blood-wet window through which his "patients"
would look. To turn each death anonymous, communal—

"Passenger," wrote Robespierre's epitaph, "lament not his fate,
for, were he living,
thou would'st be dead." Insert yourself

inside this window. Crowds
pushing against soldiers, shrubbery, platforms, crowds
looking and feeling at another
just like themselves.

            I am a man because I suffer,
the thin gas voice leaks inside the chamber, or is it,

I am a man because I make others
suffer in my place?

                        *

        How much *enough* to call it evidence?

        I thought my father would faint when he heard the results.

        The insides seamed as if with. The diamond of the flesh turned into,
        turned out of, it was hard to tell.

        You have to imagine, the doctors said.
        To spend an afternoon combing these words. To walk

        among the white pillars of the Temple of Poseidon
        looking for the name some poet etched there once
        as a kind of afterthought, rows and rows
        of white stone, and no one could find it:

        so many others had added names, dates, the pillars
        had become a kind of cemetery,

but I was desperate for the remnant, the authority.
I needed to trace my fingers through the name, to step inside of it.

How deep the eye. How deep the knife, the hand, the imagination—

And once again we took off
coat and sweater, blouse and skirt. Someone came
and washed her scent off. The oils of her hair.
How much further and still be her?
They put a knife in. They took out lining
and consciousness, tissue, time, they took out speech,
then brought it back. And now

they give us another body, a littler one, and we start
the process over in reverse. The lenses, blouse, shoes, skirt,
makeup, hair oils. And added to it, the little
rubber breast padding for what's been lost—

I should have looked, like Tussaud, with my glasses
and my lock of hair.

I should have stood stretching out my hand for the perspective,
knowing it was only a thought that night that I

was the killer, I had the knife in hand, I was taking out the heart
and tongue, I was cutting off the fingers, it was me doing it,
that blood, that distance—

Nothing scraped at the floorboards. Nothing blew down and whistled
in the street. And somewhere an image
in the mind's blank cavern: the body's senseless

clawing out of color, its muds and greens and pallid lights.

You cannot tell just what the body is
or where the corruption will take it:

it is like trying to pinpoint the soul
as it animates the body: it exists, like a painting does,

between the real and imagined, where the wax itself
comes back to life.

They asked us to look
and understand the stain, the shadow on the X-ray
but the shadow was too much a shape

to be an idea as yet. We looked, and the shadow
turned into fist, a face, it blossomed
like a Japanese lotus in a dish of water, it turned
beautiful and remote, black sun around which
the ghostly others lost duration, turned themselves in orbit—

No, the doctors said. And urged us to paint

the image thickly over, keep her untouched color
and shade, hue that recalls the vivid flesh
and just its opposite, to let dirt scrub into the cracks—

After the operations, she is
not only human but the state
of working toward humanity, away from it,

while in my mind her face can be remolded to last
longer than wood, longer than stone, to last

as long as there is wax, her image always at the point
of just emerging. Let me look. Here

are the cells with their rotten codes.
Here are breasts, belly, the still-pink organs ripe and flush:

myself liquifying into the family's
deathless increase.
I can see the swelling
in armpit, groin, the milk glands ripened in the breast. Passenger:

I had no idea what it meant,
lingering alone, black-eyed in doorways—
Take off the vest. Peel off the fragments

that are left, the sweat-stained
shoes and blouse, glasses, sweater: let us trace our fingers
through the names, let us add them to us, so that later
we can take it all away.

The drumroll is echoing in the chamber. It takes me down

where so many have gathered, crowds upon crowds
for the blood-wet window
through which each citizen must look.

The crowd shudders as the cord is cut. Shock
that travels through everybody. Makes a family out of every
body. Then isolates the patient.

They held my little X-ray up to the light and.

The king is dead. Do you believe it?

Passenger: touch this pillar for a sign.

Someone has to raise the head.
Someone has to imagine the other side.

from *Witness*

Middle School

◊   ◊   ◊

I went to Cesare Pavese Middle School.
The gymnasium was a chapel dedicated to loneliness
and no one played games.
There was a stained glass window over the principal's desk
and innumerable birds flew against it,
reciting Shelley with all their might,
but it was bulletproof, and besides,
our leaders were never immortal.
The classrooms were modeled after motel rooms,
replete with stains, and in remedial cases
saucers of milk on the floor for innumerable cats,
or kittens, depending on the time of year.
In them we were expected to examine ourselves and pass.
The principal himself once jumped off the roof
at noon, to show us school spirit.
Our mascot was Twist-Tie Man.
Our team The Bitter Herbs.
Our club The Reconsiderers.
It was an honor to have gone,
though a tad strict in retrospect.
You have probably heard that we all became janitors,
sitting in basements next to boilers
reading cheap paperback books of Italian poetry,
and never sweep a thing.
Yet the world runs fine.

from *Conduit*

DON RUSS

Girl with Gerbil

◊   ◊   ◊

Out of the no-place
of her not-yet-need she dreams
herself. Unmoved face of the deep
her mirror,

she sees as much as says
I am that I am. I make me now what first
made me: love renewed, bound up,
embodied—always life come burning

back. I prepare my house—
if cardboard, straight and true, a shoebox
Kleenex-bedded, riddled through
with stately constellations.

In time—in the growing
fullness of my time—I'll know myself
in knowing another. Some other one
and only me.

from *The Cincinnati Review*

KAY RYAN

Playacting

◇   ◇   ◇

Early tribal cultures, while celebrating their rites of initiation
or sacrifice, retained a very precise and subliminal awareness
that the compulsive extremes to which they went . . . were in
essence mere playacting, even though the performance could
sometimes approach the point of death.
—W. G. Sebald, Campo Santo

Something inside says
there will be a curtain,
maybe or maybe not
some bowing, probably
no roses, but certainly
a chance to unverse
or dehearse, after all
these acts. For some
fraction of the self
has always held out, the
evidence compounding
in a bank becoming
grander and more
marble: even our
most wholehearted
acts are partial.
Therefore this small
change, unspendable,
of a different metal,
accruing in a strange

account. What could it
be for but passage out?

from *The Threepenny Review*

The Gods

◇ ◇ ◇

I always seem to have tickets
in the third or fourth balcony
(a perch for irony;
a circle of hell the Brits
tend to call "The Gods"),
and peer down from a tier
of that empyrean

at some tuxedoed insect
scrabbling on a piano.
Some nights there's a concerto,
and ranks of sound amass
until it's raining upward
(violin-bows for lightning)
from a black thundercloud.

A railing has been installed
precisely at eye level—
which leads the gaze, frustrated,
still higher to the vault
of the gilt-encrusted ceiling,
where a vaguely understood
fresco that must be good

shows nymphs or angels wrapped
in windswept drapery.
Inscribed like the gray curls
around the distant bald spot

of the eminent conductor,
great names—DA VINCI PLATO
WHITTIER DEBUSSY—

form one long signature,
fascinatingly random,
at the marble base of the dome.
It's more the well-fed gods
of philanthropy who seem
enshrined in all their funny,
decent, noble, wrong

postulates, and who haunt
these pillared concert halls,
the tinkling foyers strung
with chandeliered ideals,
having selected which
dated virtues—COURAGE
HONOR BROTHERHOOD—rated

chiseling into stone;
having been quite sure
that virtue was a thing
all men sought, the sublime
a thought subliminally
fostered by mentioning
monumentally.

All men. Never a woman's
name, of course, although
off-shoulder pulchritude
gets featured overhead—
and abstractions you might go
to women for, like BEAUTY
JUSTICE LIBERTY.

Yet at the intermission,
I generally descend
the spiral stairs unjustly
for a costly, vacant seat

I haven't paid for. Tonight
I've slipped into D9.
The lights dim. Warm applause

and, after a thrilling pause,
some stiff-necked vanities
for a moment float away—
all the gorgeous, nameless,
shifting discordances
of the world cry aloud; allowed
at last, I close my eyes.

from *The Common*

The Afterlife

◊　◊　◊

I dreamed I was in the afterlife, it was so crowded,
hordes of people, everyone seeking someone, staggering
every which way.

Who should I search for? The answer came quick: my mother.
I elbowed my way through strangers till I found her, worn,
like the day she died.

Mother, I cried, and threw my arms around her, but she
wasn't happy to see me. Her arms hung limp. Help me,
I said. You're my mother!

There are no mothers here, she said, just separate souls.
Everyone looks for their mother. I searched for mine, and found her
searching for her mother,

and so on, through the generations. Mothers, she said,
fathers, families, lovers are for the place you came from.
Here we're on our own.

Here is no help, no love, only the looking. This
is what death means, my child, this is how we pass
eternity, looking

for the love we no longer know how to give. I shuddered
myself awake. And yet—my child, she said, my child.

Or did I only dream
that word, dream within a dream?

from *River Styx*

Rain

◊　◊　◊

Rain falls on the Western world,
The coldest spring in living memory everywhere.
Winter in mid-May means the darling buds of May uncurled
On an ice-cold morgue slab, smilingly shaking loose their beautiful hair.
London rains every day anyway.
Paris is freezing. It's May, but Rome is cold.
Motorcycles being tested at the factory in Varese north of Milan are gray
Victims screaming in place and can't get out and won't get sold.

It's the recession.
It's very weird in New York.
Teen vampires are the teen obsession,
Rosebud mouths who don't use a knife and fork.
Germany at first won't save Greece, but really has to.
It's hot hot hot in parts of Texas, but rain drowns Tennessee, people die.
It's the euro. It's the Greek debt. Greece knew
It had to stop lying, but *timeo Danaos,* they're Greeks, Greeks lie.

Canoeing in the Ozarks with Pierre Leval, the rain came down so hard
The river rose twenty-three feet in the pre-dawn hours and roared.
Came the dawn, there was improbably a lifeguard,
There was a three-legged dog, the jobless numbers soared.
Dreamers woke in the dark and drowned, with time to think this can't be true.
Incomprehensible is something these things do.
They bring the Dow Jones into the Ozarks and the Ozarks into the E.U.
A raving flash flood vomits out of a raindrop. The Western world is in the I.C.U.

Entire trees rocket past. One wouldn't stand a chance in the canoe.
A three-legged dog appears, then the guy it belongs to.

You instantly knew
You'd run into a hillbilly backwoods crazy, itching to kill you.
Berlin and Athens, as the Western world flickers,
Look up blinking in the rain and lick the rain and shiver and freeze.
They open black umbrellas and put on yellow slickers
And weep sugar like honeybees dying of the bee disease.

from *The New Yorker*

Artless

◊   ◊   ◊

is my heart. A stranger
berry there never was,
tartless.

Gone sour in the sun,
in the sunroom or moonroof,
roofless.

No poetry. Plain. No
fresh, special recipe
to bless.

All I've ever made
with these hands
and life, less

substance, more rind.
Mostly rim and trim,
meatless

but making much smoke
in the old smokehouse,
no less.

Fatted from the day,
overripe and even
toxic at eve. Nonetheless,

in the end, if you must
know, if I must bend,
waistless,

to that excruciation.
No marvel, no harvest
left me speechless,

yet I find myself
somehow with heart,
aloneless.

With heart,
fighting fire with fire,
flightless.

That loud hub of us,
meat stub of us, beating us
senseless.

Spectacular in its way,
its way of not seeing,
congealing dayless

but in everydayness.
In that hopeful haunting,
(a lesser

way of saying
in darkness) there is
silencelessness

for the pressing question.
Heart, what art you?
War, star, part? Or less:

playing a part, staying apart
from the one who loves,
loveless.

from *The New Yorker*

Our Posthumous Lives

◊　◊　◊

for Mac

The first words you ever said
To me? "I like lower case Edgar
Less than upper case Edgar." Last night
I gave your book to a stranger.
I do that sometimes. I carry
A copy on the trolley or bus,
And choose some likely suspect
And pass it to them as I exit.
Don't tsk, it's not against the law—
Yet; plus, it's only between the jaws
That you exist, dead boy. I love
Your poems and wish you weren't
Weren't. Now, you're a little air
Lesson, this strange glitch attractor.
Toward the end you forgot a lot.
Apparently, if you overdo
Heroin, later, you can't smell
Madeleines. Something to do
With the sugar, Sugar? When I rub
Our lucky Krugerrand I recall
Sticking it through the hole between
Your front teeth. I miss beauty.
By the by, who was Edgar?

from *The Literary Review*

Everything That Ever Was

◇   ◇   ◇

Like a wide wake, rippling
Infinitely into the distance, everything

That ever was still is, somewhere,
Floating near the surface, nursing
Its hunger for you and me

And the now we've named
And made a place of.

Like groundswell sometimes
It surges up, claiming a little piece
Of what we stand on.

Like the wind the rains ride in on,
It sweeps across the leaves,

Pushing in past the windows
We didn't slam quickly enough.
Dark water it will take days to drain.

It surprised us last night in my sleep.
Brought food, a gift. Stood squarely

There between us, while your eyes
Danced toward mine, and my hands
Sat working a thread in my lap.

Up close, it was so thin. And when finally
You reached for me, it backed away.

Bereft, but not vanquished. After it left,
All I wanted was your broad back

To steady my limbs. Today,
Whatever it was seems slight, a trail
Of cloud rising up and off like smoke.

And the trees that watch as I write
Sway in the breeze, as if all that stirs
Under the soil is a little tickle of knowledge

The great blind roots will tease through
And push eventually past.

from *Zoland Poetry*

The Drag Queen Dies in New Castle

◊   ◊   ◊

Returning home
   at twenty-nine, you made
a bed your throne, your
   brothers carrying you
from room to room,

each one in turn holding
   the glass to your lips,
though you were the oldest
   of the brood. Buried
by the barn, you vanished,

but the church women
   bought your wigs
for the Christmas pageant
   that year, your blouses sewn
into a quilt under which

two newlyweds lay,
   skin to skin as if they
carried some sense
   of your undressing. Skirts
swayed where sheep grazed

the plow and the farmer
   reached between legs

to pull out the calf,
  fluid gushing to his feet.
On lines across town,

dresses flapped empty
  over mulch while you
kept putting on your show,
  bones undressing like
it's never over, throwing

off your last great shift
  where a fox snake sank
its teeth into a corn
  toad's back, the whole
field flush with clover.

from *The Gettysburg Review*

MARK STRAND

The Mysterious Arrival
of an Unusual Letter

◊   ◊   ◊

It had been a long day at the office and a long ride back to the small apartment where I lived. When I got there I flicked on the light and saw on the table an envelope with my name on it. Where was the clock? Where was the calendar? The handwriting was my father's, but he had been dead for forty years. As one might, I began to think that maybe, just maybe, he was alive, living a secret life somewhere nearby. How else to explain the envelope? To steady myself, I sat down, opened it, and pulled out the letter. "Dear Son," was the way it began. "Dear Son" and then nothing.

from *Poetry*

Sunflower

◊ ◊ ◊

Wind takes your hair
like a hooligan owl
and leaves a deep pocket
of dusk in your scalp.

Love without pride
is a love with no end.
You keep calling me in
to fill up your head,

but the mutinous dust
of the dead yellow field
says better not listen
to a thing with a stem.

from *Ploughshares*

The Turnpike

◇　◇　◇

. . . an expansion,
Like gold to airy thinness beat . . .

You away, and me on the Peter Pan
　　　　heading home from my own required remove,
I'm drawn by the window's broad reflection,
　　　　the traffic passing along it like a nerve—

an endless charge of cars inside the pane:
　　　　the voltage of the real; though as they go
sliding down its long, ethereal sheen
　　　　where the solid world softens into flow

they take on the ghostly substance of a dream
　　　　or, rather, what we picture dreams to be
since when we're in them they are what we seem,
　　　　and cause us joy or pain as vividly

as the lives we think we live between the lines
　　　　that imprint us and we pass between.
Here, the world inverts. Shades materialize
　　　　and cars speeding left expand a breach

that transports into doubles on the right,
　　　　and those in transit opposite condense
their mirror selves in a second teeming flight
　　　　as if our lightship bus could break such bonds

and matter shatter. Like all things physical
        it's a conjure of parts and energies,
a Never Land of haunts inside the skull,
          though saying so won't prevent this child's cries

from jolting with their needful disturbance,
        or the aging woman across the aisle
from leaning in her slackened, palpable face—
        comically, mildly—till the infant calms.

If as scientists say we are like hurled stones,
        as bounded and bound, dear, by material,
and that our minds resolve into a mist
        we thinly feel to be the actual,

then who's to say the rock is not the air
        it hurtles through, observed from deeper in,
not above. So you and I circuit there,
        firing the inexhaustible engine.

from *Southwest Review*

NATASHA TRETHEWEY

Dr. Samuel Adolphus Cartwright on Dissecting the White Negro, 1851

◊   ◊   ◊

To strip from the flesh
    the specious skin; to weigh
        in the brainpan
    seeds of white
pepper; to find in the body
    its own diminishment—
        blood-deep
    and definite; to measure the heft
of lack; to make of the work of faith
    the work of science, evidence
        the word of God: Canaan
be the *servant of servants*; thus
    to know the truth
        of this: (this derelict
corpus, a dark compendium, this
    atavistic assemblage—flatter
feet, bowed legs, a shorter neck) so
    deep the tincture
        —*see it!*—
we still know white from not.

from *New England Review*

From "The Split"

◊   ◊   ◊

'Bye, kid in first grade on your paddle cart.

'Bye, Lorraine, Outward Bound in the snow.

'Bye, motorcycle David.

'Bye, you bright spirits, born of my friends. Jimmy. Natalie.

'Bye, beautiful one, your father said your pink skin would be tender, I was
   afraid for you.

'Bye, one's devoted mother, another's devoted son.

'Bye to Playboy Club Bill, to the Roxy Bill, to the Bill going aft with the cross.

'Bye, dickering friend to Sonja, I wanted to show you up.

'Bye Dad, 'bye Mom.

'Bye, Duncan's dancing bear shining, shining.

'Bye, great dogs I have known. Cats. Raccoon I hit.

'Bye to Bob Liberty, you must be gone.

'Bye to the beggar no more on his corner.

'Bye, Ben, sparklers and flowers, the lamp of the music.

'Bye, Barbara Latham, Abinata, Ray Yoshida. 'Bye, Gelsy.

'Bye, Meldrum and Carrel, Gladys, Olive C. 'Bye, May and Winslow. My lovely
first cousin.

'Bye to the husband who was the best wife.

'Bye to those I fear dead.

I know you all in his absence tonight.

I know you all in his absence tonight.

from *The New Yorker*

FRANZ WRIGHT

The Lesson

◇　◇　◇

Say you finally make it home after a particularly arduous day in eighth grade to find the front door standing open and the furniture gone, and wander awhile through the oddly spacious rooms like a paralytic drowning in the bathtub while the nurse goes to answer the phone. True, you were never the best behaved little girl who ever lived; still, it seems fair to say that this is the wrong surprise party for you. A little later, looking down from somewhere near the ceiling, you observe yourself letting a cheap unwashed wine glass slip from your fingers, bending over to select a large section of it from the kitchen floor and beginning, with intense focus and precision, to inscribe a fairly serious gash in your left wrist. That doesn't work out so well. Locating a dish towel, though, does keep you occupied, then cleaning up the mess you've made. And you refuse to cry. Smart move, you hear a voice say quite distinctly. You might really need those tears someday. And you have been telling yourself the same thing all your life.

from *The Kenyon Review*

Minding Rites

◇   ◇   ◇

This guy I know, a rabbi, Friday nights,
on his way home before sunset in winter,
always stops at a florist or bodega
and buys a bunch of flowers for his wife.

Every week the same, a ritual,
regardless of her mood that morning, fresh
upsets at work, or snarling on the bridge;
he brings her roses wrapped in cellophane.

But isn't there a ring of hokiness
in that? Why should a good man make a show
of his devotion? Some things go unspoken;
some things get tested on the real world,

and isn't that the place that matters most?
So when you told me I should bring you flowers,
I laughed, "But don't I show my feelings more
in dog-walks, diapers, and rewiring lamps?"

The flowers, I learned later, weren't for wooing,
not for affection in long marriage, but
for something seeded even deeper down,
through frost heaves, and which might be, roughly, peace.

(It's funny that I just assumed romance.)
Now there's no peace with us, I wonder what

they might have meant to you, those simple tokens,
holding in sight what no rite can grow back.

from *New Ohio Review*

Restoration Ode

◇　◇　◇

What tends toward orbit and return,
comets and melodies, robins and trash trucks
restore us. What would be an arrow, a dove
to pierce our hearts restores us. Restore us

minutes clustered like nursing baby bats
and minutes that are shards of glass. Mountains
that are vapor, mice living in cathedrals
and the heft and lightness of snow restore us.

One hope inside dread, "Oh what the hell"
inside "I can't" like a pearl inside a cake
of soap, life in lust in loss, and the tub
filled with dirt in the backyard restore us.

Sunflowers, let me wait, let me please
see the bridge again from my smacked-up
desk on Euclid, jog by the Black Angel
without begging, dream without thrashing.

Let us be quick and accurate with the knife.
And everything that dashes restore us,
salmon, shadows buzzing in the wind,
wren trapped in the atrium, and all

that stills at last, my friend's cat
a pile of leaves after much practice,
and ash beneath the grate, last ember
winked shut restore us. And the one who comes

out from the back wiping his hands on a rag,
saying, "Who knows, there might be a chance."
And one more undestroyed, knocked-down nest
stitched with cellophane and dental floss,

one more gift to gently shake
and one more guess and one more chance.

from *The Gettysburg Review*

Expecting

◊   ◊   ◊

Grave, my wife lies back, hands cross
her chest, while the doctor searches early
for your heartbeat, peach pit, unripe

plum—pulls out the world's worst
boom box, a Mr. Microphone, to broadcast
your mother's lifting belly.

The whoosh and bellows of mama's body
and beneath it: nothing. Beneath
the slow stutter of her heart: nothing.

The doctor trying again to find you, fragile
fern, snowflake. Nothing.
After, my wife will say, in fear,

impatient, she went beyond her body,
this tiny room, into the ether—
for now, we spelunk for you one last time

lost canary, miner of coal
and chalk, lungs not yet black—
I hold my wife's feet to keep her here—

and me—trying not to dive starboard
to seek you in the dark water. And there
it is: faint, an echo, faster and further

away than mother's, all beat box
and fuzzy feedback. You are like hearing
hip-hop for the first time—power

hijacked from a lamppost—all promise.
You couldn't sound better, break-
dancer, my favorite song bumping

from a passing car. You've snuck
into the club underage and stayed!
Only later, much, will your mother

begin to believe your drumming
in the distance—my Kansas City
and Congo Square, this jazz band

vamping on inside her.

from *The New Yorker*

CONTRIBUTORS' NOTES AND COMMENTS

SHERMAN ALEXIE was born in 1966 and grew up on the Spokane Indian Reservation. His first collection of stories, *The Lone Ranger and Tonto Fistfight in Heaven* (Atlantic Monthly Press, 1993), won a PEN/ Hemingway Award. In collaboration with Chris Eyre, a Cheyenne/ Arapaho Indian filmmaker, Alexie adapted a story from that book, "This Is What It Means to Say Phoenix, Arizona," into the screenplay for the movie *Smoke Signals*. His most recent books are the poetry collection *Face,* from Hanging Loose Press (2009), and *War Dances,* stories and poems from Grove Press (2009). He is lucky enough to be a full-time writer and lives with his family in Seattle.

Of "Terminal Nostalgia," Alexie writes: "For such a young country, the United States is intensely nostalgic. And Internet culture—with its endless remixes of pop culture—is even more nostalgic. As for the particular brand of nostalgia that afflicts Native Americans? Well, it has a lot to do with romanticizing pre-Columbian culture. Thinking about all this, I thought I'd write a ghazal (a seventh-century Arabic poetic form) that combined American pop culture nostalgia with Native American cultural nostalgia. The result is, I believe, funny and sad at the same time, although, when I've performed it live, it seems that people are afraid to laugh."

KAREN LEONA ANDERSON was born in Manchester, Connecticut, in 1973. She is the author of *Punish honey* (Carolina Wren Press, 2009) and is an assistant professor of English at St. Mary's College of Maryland.

Of "Receipt: Midway Entertainment Presents," Anderson writes: "A few years ago, I started using my cash register receipts as occasions for poems, a practice that has proven to be both revelatory and embarrassing. This poem in particular was based on a ticket stub from the county fair in St. Mary's County, Maryland, which is a lot like the fairs I used to go to in eastern Connecticut and southwestern Minnesota. I'm a former 4-H member (I mostly entered marigolds and cake), and I always liked the mobility of being at the fair—moving like money from the surreal mash-up of those intense local contests to that other economy in the parallel universe of the midway."

RAE ARMANTROUT was born in Vallejo, California, in 1947. She teaches in the Literature Department at the University of California, San Diego. Her most recent books are *Money Shot* (2011), *Versed* (2009), which won the 2010 Pulitzer Prize, and *Next Life* (2007), all from Wesleyan University Press. *Just Saying,* the manuscript containing "Accounts," will be published by Wesleyan in 2013.

Armantrout writes: "Like many of us, I have been fascinated with physics, as I encountered it in popular books such as Brian Greene's, for many years. In the summer of 2010, I invited a professor of astrophysics at UC San Diego, Brian Keating, to lunch, hoping he could help me understand the origin of matter in the early universe. The poem is not a transcript of our conversation, but rather an absurdist account of my attempts to visualize what Brian was saying. At times it takes the form of two voices, one correcting the other. Such visualizations and corrections could go on indefinitely."

JULIANNA BAGGOTT was born in Wilmington, Delaware, in 1969. She is the author of eighteen books, mostly novels, under her own name as well as the pen names Bridget Asher and N. E. Bode. Three of her books are collections of poetry: *This Country of Mothers* (Southern Illinois University Press, 2001), *Lizzie Borden in Love* (SIU Press, 2006), and *Compulsions of Silkworms and Bees* (Pleiades Press/Louisiana State University Press, 2007), which is a manual on how to write poems, written in poems. An earlier version of the poem in these pages appeared in a desktop calendar published by Alhambra. Baggott's most recent novel, *Pure* (Hachette, 2012), is the first in a postapocalyptic trilogy. She teaches at Florida State University.

Of "For Furious Nursing Baby," Baggott writes: "First, I should confess: I can be contrary. I wrote a poem called 'Q and A: Why I Don't Write Formal Poetry,' and realized, by the end of it, that I'd challenged myself into some kind of formal duel. I started writing sonnets. At first, I was very strict then loosened. 'For Furious Nursing Baby' was originally a sonnet—you can still hear it echoing—that eventually simply looked too confined and bound-down on the page. The poem is about the wildness of a nursing baby—a poem undeniably of the flesh. I felt compelled to unclasp the lines . . . and so now, when I look at it on the page, it appears sprung loose, as the flesh of nursing breasts tend to do when unbound, unclasped."

DAVID BAKER was born in Bangor, Maine, grew up in Jefferson City, Missouri, and has lived since 1984 in Granville, Ohio. He teaches at Denison University, where he holds the Thomas B. Fordham endowed chair of English, and also teaches regularly in the MFA program at Warren Wilson College. The latest of his fourteen books are *Talk Poetry: Poems and Interviews with Nine American Poets* (University of Arkansas Press, 2012) and *Never-Ending Birds* (W. W. Norton), winner of the 2011 Theodore Roethke Memorial Poetry Prize. He is poetry editor of *The Kenyon Review.*

Of "Outside," Baker writes: "Where does art live? It tends to live indoors—inside massive buildings like mansions, monasteries, and museums, or inside fussy little buildings like galleries and academies. But in my small village in Ohio art also lives in trees, in reconstituted toilets, out in the yard, even in the air—on the property of one citizen, who lives inside my poem 'Outside.' A few years ago this fellow moved himself onto an acre of his family's old farm site, outside, I mean; when the weather is bad he stays in farm buildings. And he has moved his utilities outside, his sink and stove and such, and some of these also house his art.

"By outsider art we usually mean the works created by people who are not typical or mainstream artists, whose work may be folk art, or whose reputations are not respectable within the cozy confines of 'fine art.' Outsiders are outside the field. But my neighbor is an actual outsider. He lives outside in a real farmyard. His art lives outside. And this is where he is at home.

"My poem barely touches upon all the idiosyncratic, inventive, and nonce creations he has made. Some are functional. Some are 'pure' art. And my friend finds no difference between function and purity, between his living and his making, or between his inner world and his outside existence."

RICK BAROT was born in the Philippines and grew up in the San Francisco Bay Area. He has received fellowships from the National Endowment for the Árts, the Artist Trust of Washington, the Civitella Ranieri Foundation, and Stanford University. He has published two books of poetry with Sarabande Books: *The Darker Fall* (2002) and *Want* (2008), which won the 2009 Grub Street Book Prize. He lives in Tacoma, Washington, and teaches at Pacific Lutheran University and at Warren Wilson College.

Of "Child Holding Potato," Barot writes: "The painting referred to in the poem's title is by Giovanni Bellini, in the Metropolitan Museum in New York City. Recently, I was at a dinner party and discovered that the woman sitting across from me had worked as a docent for decades at the Met. It was fun to talk to someone who could conjure up in her own mind the paintings that I loved at the museum. When I mentioned the Bellini, she said she didn't think it was a potato in the child's hand, though she wasn't sure what it was. I made a mental note then to look into books about Bellini and find out exactly what the object is. To my eye the object had looked like a gold potato, though I suppose now that it could be any number of other things: another tuber, maybe, or a pear, or a stone. I still haven't looked it up. And, in any case, the misreading now seems an important part of my relationship with the painting and the poem that came out of it. In the state of mind I was in while looking at the painting, a pear or a stone would have been just as dire as a funny little potato."

REGINALD DWAYNE BETTS was born in Oceanside, California, in 1980. He is the author of a memoir, *A Question of Freedom* (Avery/Penguin, 2009), and a poetry collection, *Shahid Reads His Own Palm* (Alice James Books, 2010). He has received fellowships from the Radcliffe Institute for Advanced Studies, the Open Society Institute, Bread Loaf Writers' Conference, and Warren Wilson College. As national spokesperson for the Campaign for Youth Justice, Betts writes and lectures about the impact of mass incarceration on American society. Married, the father of two sons, he lives in Clinton, Maryland.

Betts writes: " 'At the End of Life, a Secret' started with a story I read about a dying person, weight that was unaccounted for, and a claim that this weight was that of the soul. At the time the Supreme Court was hearing, or had just heard, *Steven Spears v. the United States,* the case that declared unconstitutional the 100:1 disparity in crack-cocaine sentences and powder cocaine sentences. The case had me thinking about the weight of crack, both the physical weight and the weight of its impact on the communities I grew up in and on the American legal system. As I worked on the poem those two things collided—though not until the very end. While the poem might seem the product of a plan, that is a mirage of hindsight. The end product is always an artifact, implying a logic that the poet composing it did not yet have. Composition, in my experience, is play, is riffing, is taking an image (in this case the man working with the cadaver) and working it over and beyond the idea until I land at a place that I didn't expect."

FRANK BIDART was born in Bakersfield, California, in 1939. He didn't escape until 1957, when he began to study at the University of California, Riverside. "Escape" is an exaggeration; childhood and youth take too long, perhaps everywhere. He began graduate work at Harvard in 1962, studying with Reuben Brower and Robert Lowell. His books include *Star Dust* (2005) and *Desire* (1997), both from Farrar, Straus and Giroux. He is the coeditor of Robert Lowell's *Collected Poems* (2003) and has taught at Wellesley College since 1972. Rosanna Warren has called him an "occult Poundian," adding: "At every level of Bidart's poems—syntactic, prosodic, prepositional—contradiction provides the emotional fuel." Bidart lives in Cambridge, Massachusetts.

Of "Of His Bones Are Coral Made," Bidart writes: "I've written little prose about poetry, but can't seem to stop writing poems about poetics. Narrative is the Elephant in the Room when most people discuss poetry. Narrative was never a crucial element in the poetics surrounding the birth of Modernism, though the great works of Modernism, from *The Waste Land* to the *Cantos* to 'Home Burial,' *Paterson,* and beyond, are built on a brilliant sense of the power of narrative. What Modernism added was the power gained when you know what to leave out. Narrative is the ghost scaffolding that gives spine to the great works that haunt the twentieth century.

"A writer is caught by certain narratives, certain characters, and not by others. Prufrock is relevant to our sense of Eliot. He could be a character in Pound's sequence *Hugh Selwyn Mauberly,* but if he were, it would be without the identification, the sympathy and agony. Eliot had to go on to Gerontion and Sweeney and Tiresias, each trailing a ghost narrative. They are as crucial to Eliot's vision as Bloom and Stephen Daedalus are to the vision, the sense of the nature of the world, of Joyce.

"In my poem, *'the creature smothered in death clothes'* is Herbert White, the title character in the first poem in my first book; 'the woman' two stanzas down is Ellen West, from the second.

"Two more allusions. The 'burning / fountain' refers to this passage in Shelley's poem 'Adonais,' his elegy for Keats:

He wakes or sleeps with the enduring dead;
Thou canst not soar where he is sitting now.—
Dust to the dust! but the pure spirit shall flow
Back to the burning fountain whence it came,
A portion of the Eternal, which must glow
Through time and change, unquenchably the same. . . .

"The 'burning fountain' is a metaphor for the power that generates, that fuels and animates life. It is the title of a book about the poetic imagination by Philip Wheelwright, who taught me philosophy as an undergraduate (*The Burning Fountain,* Indiana University Press, 1954).

"My poem's title comes from one of Shakespeare's greatest short lyrics, in *The Tempest*:

Full fathom five thy father lies;
    Of his bones are coral made:
Those are pearls that were his eyes:
    Nothing of him that doth fade,
But doth suffer a sea-change
Into something rich and strange.

"My poem is about transformation, the bones of the poet made up out of the materials, the detritus of the world, that he or she has not only gathered but transformed and been transformed by."

BRUCE BOND was born in Pasadena, California, in 1954. His collections of poetry include *Choir of the Wells* (a tetralogy of new books; Etruscan Press, 2013), *The Visible* (Louisiana State University Press, 2012), *Peal* (Etruscan Press, 2009), *Blind Rain* (Louisiana State University Press, 2008), *Cinder* (Etruscan Press, 2003), *The Throats of Narcissus* (University of Arkansas Press, 2001), *Radiography* (BOA Editions, 1997), *The Anteroom of Paradise* (QRL, 1991), and *Independence Days* (Woodley Press, 1990). He has received fellowships from the National Endowment for the Arts, the Texas Institute of the Arts, and the Institute for the Advancement of the Arts. He is a Regents Professor of English at the University of North Texas and poetry editor for *American Literary Review.* His work has appeared twice previously in *The Best American Poetry.*

Of "Pill," Bond writes: "I recall a particular morning-after, when I was in the shower at Pomona College some thirty-seven years ago. It struck me then that feeling high is highly overrated, largely because it alters and destabilizes the norm. What if it were the norm? What would people pay for the chance of two minutes of sobriety? What wouldn't they pay? But then this poem is one that I could have written only much later in life. For now sobriety suggests to me that post-midlife turn back to the dailiness of one's world and one's finitude within it. Suffice it to say that I have made my share of mistakes. Join the club, say my mistakes. If, beyond the bare necessities required to survive, anxiety is the fundamental human problem (which I believe it is), then the courage to regard the fullness of one's nature remains its central difficulty. And if conversation with (and transfiguration of) the wounded places is what experience craves, that does not preclude its craving of denial and the grandiosity of the child. To be high is to stand above the real somehow, above others. But to be ground level is to acknowledge a bit more of both our connectivity and our aloneness: as Stevens put it, our 'island solitude, unsponsored, free, / Of that wide water, inescapable.' So much depends upon those twin commas after 'free' and 'water.' A confession: I have had my problems with sleep. Now, oddly, when I lie down, I say the word 'nothing' in my head. That's where I came from, where I'm headed. It's OK. I say. Nothing. And then I feel a little gratitude. And then I fall."

STEPHANIE BROWN was born in 1961 in Pasadena, California, and grew up in Newport Beach. She has degrees from Boston University, the University of Iowa Writers' Workshop, and the University of California at Berkeley. She is the author of two books of poetry, *Domestic Interior* (University of Pittsburgh Press, 2008) and *Allegory of the Supermarket* (University of Georgia Press, 1998). She has received fellowships from the National Endowment for the Arts and the Bread Loaf Writers' Conference. A curator of the Casa Romantica Reading Series for poets and fiction writers in San Clemente, California, from 2004 to 2010, she has taught creative writing at the University of California, Irvine, and the University of Redlands, but has primarily made her living as a librarian and library manager. She is currently a regional branch manager for OC Public Libraries in Southern California. She is also a book review editor of the online journal *Connotation Press: An Online Artifact* and poetry editor of the *Zócalo Public Square* website.

Of "Notre Dame," Brown writes: "I'm always looking for ways to make myself write. The first draft is the hardest. One year I placed a random list of A–Z words in my Outlook reminder box at work, to have a daily prompt pop up for twenty-six workdays. On the third day, the word was 'cathedral,' and this was the poem I wrote from that prompt. This poem wrote itself very much as it exists now on the page. The moment of discovery in the writing was when I got to the line that begins, 'It was a terrible summer.' Until that point, I was writing the poem as if angels were its subject, but then I saw that it was meant to go in a different direction and I let it go there. I didn't do much revision, though I took out some stage-setting lines at the beginning. The title came last. I couldn't call it 'Cathedral' because that made me think of Raymond Carver's seminal book of short stories, *Cathedral*. I toyed with the idea of calling it 'Paris' but ultimately chose 'Notre Dame,' because the poem is about faith more than anything else, and Notre Dame stands as a symbol of faith. I do love the 'thoughtful gargoyle' at the top, who rests his chin in his hand and contemplates the city spread out before him. When I think of Notre Dame, I think of the rose window, the candles burning, the beautiful façade, and that gargoyle."

ANNE CARSON was born in Toronto, Canada, in 1950. She teaches ancient Greek at various places, now at New York University. Her most recent book is *Nox* (New Directions, 2011).

Carson writes: " 'Sonnet of Exemplary Sentences' was part of a sonnet cycle I wrote once when invited to Harvard to give a lecture on pronouns. The sonnets were performed as part of a collaborative composition that included choreography by three dancers from the Merce Cunningham Company—Rashaun Mitchell, Julie Cunningham, and Andrea Weber—with sound design by Stephanie Rowden and video by Sadie Wilcox. Harvard was baffled but appreciative."

JENNIFER CHANG was born in New Brunswick, New Jersey, in 1976, and was educated at the University of Chicago and the University of Virginia. She is the author of *The History of Anonymity* (*VQR* Poetry Series/University of Georgia Press, 2008). She cochairs the advisory board of Kundiman, a nonprofit organization that supports and promotes Asian-American poetry, and is an assistant professor of creative writing and literature at Bowling Green State University.

Of "Dorothy Wordsworth," Chang writes: "The first draft came swiftly, and then I spent nearly two years revising it. I'd written it for National Poetry Month's 'write a poem a day' challenge, which I'd never participated in before, but I was being wooed by a non-poet trying to impress me by gamely writing poems and I was wooing as a poet trying to impress him by writing obstreperously. The title was initially

'Wordsworth' and I had the word 'jaunty' somewhere. It was pure dreck, not jaunty at all, but I liked the first line and took the trouble of revising it into quatrains. Later, after further ill-fated tweaking, I made the poem worse, retitling it 'Ode: Intimations of Immortality,' and shared it at a reading, where no one laughed or sighed or knew what to make of it.

"I had been thinking a lot about Dorothy Wordsworth, too. 'I do not remember this day,' reads one entry from *Alfoxden Journal*, which is one way of staying quiet. I couldn't help comparing this to the Dorothy we find in 'Tintern Abbey,' silently absorbing her brother's lyric exertions. What did she remember of *that* day? I wanted more words from her, from myself, but I was done. The poem was kaput. Until one afternoon, sparked by impertinence, a good impetus for revision, I surprised myself by taking the poem out and arriving at a new ending and title. And then I stuck my own name on it!"

JOSEPH CHAPMAN was born in Charlotte, North Carolina, in 1982. He attended the University of North Carolina at Chapel Hill, where he earned a BA in English, and the University of Virginia, where he earned an MFA in poetry writing. From 2007 to 2008, he served as poetry editor for *Meridian* magazine. He lives in Ann Arbor, Michigan, with his wife, Julia Hansen.

Chapman writes: "When the editors of *The Cincinnati Review* originally took 'Sparrow,' they invited me to write a brief explanation of the poem's genesis. I wrote about the sources of the poem—St. John of the Cross's *Ascent of Mount Carmel* and the Psalms—and the way the poem's borrowed language animates a speaker who then becomes language again.

"Rereading the poem more than a year later, I'm less fascinated by its sources. Instead I find myself drawn to its surfaces: the oil spot becoming a closed garden becoming a sealed fountain; the dark habit of St. John of the Cross that doubles as a rib cage and a bird's oily, feathered wings. The end of the poem remains startling to me, which is a good thing, I guess. Every image in the poem metamorphoses into 'words / & the Sparrow.' That shift is my attempt at a fancy enactment of the simple truth that language consumes everything. That God consumes us.

"I couldn't have said any of this after I initially wrote the poem. But I think it's important that the poem wants to preserve the life of all things outside us, including the things we imagine and the word we imagine them with. Even though I can picture the exact parking garage in which

I set the poem—the Water Street garage near the downtown mall in Charlottesville—the sparrow and the language I used in the poem are no longer my own, if they ever were."

HEATHER CHRISTLE was born in Wolfeboro, New Hampshire, in 1980. She is the author of three poetry collections: *What Is Amazing* (Wesleyan University Press, 2012), *The Trees The Trees* (Octopus Books, 2011), and *The Difficult Farm* (Octopus Books, 2009). She has taught at the University of Massachusetts, Amherst, and at Emory University, where she was the 2009–2011 Poetry Writing Fellow. She is the web editor for *jubilat* and lives in Western Massachusetts with her husband, Christopher DeWeese, a poet, and her cat, Hastings.

Of "BASIC," Christle writes: "This poem occurred to me fairly quickly, though not all at once. It began (as things often do) with an image/premise, and then grew through the imagination of consequences. The initial image came from a childhood memory I have of learning how to use Logo, a computer programming language designed as an educational tool. We'd type in 'FD 100 RT 120 FD 100 RT 120' and this little turtle icon would draw a triangle. Magic! I chose the name of a different programming language—BASIC—as the title, because it had a few more shades of meaning to it. For me, the heart of this poem lies in its belief that whatever happens (beginning on the screen, and then moving out into the world) is the result of the program's design. I would like to write a program that makes people cry, but I do not know how, and so instead I have to write poems."

HENRI COLE was born in Fukuoka, Japan, in 1956. He has published eight collections of poetry, including *Middle Earth*. He has received the Kingsley Tufts Award, the Rome Prize, the Berlin Prize, a Guggenheim Fellowship, and the Lenore Marshall Award. His most recent collection is *Touch* (Farrar, Straus and Giroux, 2011). He teaches at Ohio State University and is poetry editor of *The New Republic*. He lives in Boston.

Of "Broom," Cole writes: "I wrote this poem after the death of Mother, a Frenchwoman who came to this country as a young military bride. Though she spent sixty years trying to be an American, at the end of her life she became a Frenchwoman again, only speaking the language I love. I think of her every day."

BILLY COLLINS was born in the French Hospital in New York City in 1941. He was an undergraduate at Holy Cross College and received his PhD from the University of California, Riverside. His books of poetry include *Horoscopes for the Dead* (Random House, 2011), *Ballistics* (Random House, 2008), *The Trouble with Poetry and Other Poems* (Random House, 2005), a collection of haiku titled *She Was Just Seventeen* (Modern Haiku Press, 2006), *Nine Horses* (Random House, 2002), *Sailing Alone Around the Room: New and Selected Poems* (Random House, 2001), *Picnic, Lightning* (University of Pittsburgh Press, 1998), *The Art of Drowning* (University of Pittsburgh Press, 1995), and *Questions About Angels* (William Morrow, 1991), which was selected for the National Poetry Series by Edward Hirsch and reprinted by the University of Pittsburgh Press in 1999. He is the editor of *Poetry 180: A Turning Back to Poetry* (Random House, 2003) and *180 More: Extraordinary Poems for Everyday* (Random House, 2005). He is a Distinguished Professor of English at Lehman College (City University of New York) and a Distinguished Fellow of the Winter Park Institute of Rollins College. A frequent contributor and former guest editor of *The Best American Poetry* series, he was appointed United States Poet Laureate 2001–2003 and served as New York State Poet 2004–2006. He also edited *Bright Wings: An Illustrated Anthology of Poems About Birds,* illustrated by David Sibley (Columbia University Press, 2010).

Of "Delivery," Collins writes: "Here we are back at lyric poetry's oldest subject, only instead of the hooded no-face ready to cut you down with a scythe, we have a delivery truck. To associate a vehicle with death is nothing new; whether the fancy is for a sweet chariot, a ferryboat across Stygian waters, or a horse-drawn carriage heading toward 'Eternity,' we like to think of dying as a journey, especially one that begins with someone picking us up and taking us somewhere. It beats being alone. Here, the truck is only delivering the news, but even that is too frightening for 'the speaker,' who substitutes the benign image of a *drawing* of a truck and then gets busy adding some endearing boyhood details. As I look back at the poem, it seems nothing more than a futile attempt at avoidance, but at least it echoes a theme both noble and ancient. I don't know if I had in mind Yannis Ritsos's amazing poem 'Miniature,' in which death arrives in a fairy-tale carriage whose wheels are made of lemon slices, but even if I wasn't, my poem lies uneasily in that poem's shadow."

PETER COOLEY was born in Detroit in 1940 and grew up there and in the suburbs of the city. He is a graduate of Shimer College, the University of Chicago, and the Writers' Workshop at the University of Iowa.

From 1970 to 2000 he was poetry editor of *North American Review*. Since 1975 he has lived in New Orleans, where he teaches creative writing at Tulane University. He has published eight volumes of poetry, seven of them with Carnegie Mellon University Press. That press will soon release his latest, *Night Bus to the Afterlife*. He is currently finishing a volume of ekphrastic poems on Rembrandt, Rodin, and Michelangelo.

Cooley writes: "I am irritated by our contemporary mania for mandating 'relevant' topics for the poet. For years I have been told I should be writing about New Orleans since it is such an interesting city. When Katrina hit and people found out my wife and I stayed in town for the hurricane, I was told I should be writing about the storm. I have been warned repeatedly that I should not be writing about religious subjects unless I express healthy disbelief. This poem is my perverse way of answering clarion calls for poems about tourism and disaster but still maintaining 'I'll write religious poems if I damn well please.'"

EDUARDO C. CORRAL was born in Casa Grande, Arizona, in 1973. His work has been honored with a "Discovery"/*The Nation* award and residencies from Yaddo and from the MacDowell Colony. He is the recipient of a 2011 Whiting Writers' Award. *Slow Lightning,* his first book, won the 2011 Yale Series of Younger Poets competition. He lives in New York City.

Of "To the Angelbeast," Corral writes: "The poem is dedicated to Arthur Russell, a musician/composer who died from AIDS in 1992. Formally trained as a cellist, Russell worked in many genres (disco, classical, rock, folk, experimental) but his cello-centric compositions are the songs that haunt me. In songs like 'A Sudden Chill,' 'Losing My Taste for the Night Life,' and 'Another Thought,' the cello becomes an animal-like presence that devours everything: melody, lyrics, voice. Everything but death."

ERICA DAWSON was born in Columbia, Maryland, in 1979. Her poems have appeared in *The Best American Poetry 2008, Barrow Street, Birmingham Poetry Review, Blackbird,* and *Harvard Review.* Her collection of poems, *Big-Eyed Afraid* (The Waywiser Press, 2007), won the 2006 Anthony Hecht Prize. *Contemporary Poetry Review* named it the Best Debut of 2007. An assistant professor of English at the University of Tampa, she serves as poetry editor for *Tampa Review* and teaches in the university's new low-residency MFA program.

Dawson writes: "'Back Matter' exists because someone calls me 'street,' perhaps too much for poetry with a capital P. Insert the wipe-your-hands-clean gesture and the shrug-it-off neck cracking.

"Irritated (understatement), I sit down to write 'Back Matter.' I'll just say the process involves the inability to read your handwriting on last night's draft. I conflate a small narrative in Cincinnati, weaving in various definitions of the word 'back.' With the narrative and countless denotations and connotations in my head, I try capturing moments when I'm part of the world with my back to it at the same time—in that cage of loneliness."

STEPHEN DUNN was born in Forest Hills, New York, in 1939 and is a distinguished professor (emeritus) of creative writing at Richard Stockton College of New Jersey. A graduate of Hofstra and Syracuse Universities, he is the author of *Walking Light* (BOA Editions, 2001), a book of essays and memoirs, and of sixteen books of poetry, including *Here and Now* (W. W. Norton, 2011, in which "The Imagined" appears). *Different Hours* (W. W. Norton, 2000) won the Pulitzer Prize. He has received fellowship awards from the Guggenheim and Rockefeller Foundations.

Dunn writes: "I began 'The Imagined' at Yaddo in the summer of 2010, and 'finished' it a few weeks later. At this point the poem consisted of its first half, with which I was somewhat but not fully pleased. A few days later I gave an 'imagined man' to the woman. This seemed not only fair, but finally truer to the likelihood of my concerns. For a while, the poem ended with 'just the two of you,' which I still believe could be a satisfactory ending. But on revisiting the poem, I added the last three lines, then crossed them out, then put them back in again.

"When I've read this poem at readings, very solemn-faced women in the audience seem to be registering disapproval with the first half of the poem. Their demeanor changes in the second half—many seem delighted that their secret man has been acknowledged and identified."

ELAINE EQUI was born in Oak Park, Illinois, in 1953. She has published six books with Coffee House Press. They include *Voice-Over* (1998), which won a San Francisco State Poetry Award; *Ripple Effect: New and Selected Poems* (2007), which was a finalist for the *Los Angeles Times* Book Prize and the Griffin Poetry Prize; and most recently, *Click and Clone* (2011). She teaches at New York University and in the MFA programs at the New School and City College. She lives in New York City.

Of "A Story Begins," Equi writes: "I like to write about reading, to reflect on how we become absorbed in books, and how in a strange way, books read us—call to us at particular moments. I was especially frustrated when I wrote this poem because it was summer, my apartment was undergoing a seemingly endless renovation, and I couldn't find a novel, mystery, or any kind of book to lose myself in. Even the most outlandish and exotic narratives sounded contrived and predictable. In the end, I gave up altogether on the idea of literary escapism. Instead, I opted to read a number of poets known for their pessimism, spleen, and generally grouchy tone. This proved to be quite entertaining and, in fact, helped me write several new poems, including this one."

ROBERT GIBB was born in 1946 in the steel town of Homestead, Pennsylvania. He is the author of eight books of poetry: *The Names of the Earth in Summer* (Stone Country, 1983), *The Winter House* (University of Missouri Press, 1984), *Momentary Days* (Walt Whitman Center, 1989), *Fugue for a Late Snow* (University of Missouri Press, 1993), *The Origins of Evening* (W. W. Norton, 1997), *The Burning World* (University of Arkansas Press, 2004), *World over Water* (University of Arkansas Press, 2007), and *What the Heart Can Bear: Selected and Uncollected Poems, 1979–1993* (Autumn House Press, 2009). He has won two fellowships from the National Endowment for the Arts. Two new books will appear in 2012: *Sheet Music* (Autumn House Press), which includes "Spirit in the Dark," and *The Empty Loom* (University of Arkansas Press). He lives on New Homestead Hill above the Monongahela River.

Gibb writes: "'Spirit in the Dark' details an instance of 'another world's intrusion into this one,' to borrow from a character in *The Crying of Lot 49*. The encounter took place late one night in an old house partitioned into apartments. We'd plated the second side of the Ninth Symphony and as the final movement began building toward the choral 'Ode to Joy,' whatever it was—ghost, spirit—entered from the hallway. Somber, it seemed drawn by the music, moving slowly toward the record player, in front of which it hovered and then, for whatever reason, simply withdrew again, leaving us—but leaving us how? Hadn't we just witnessed the inexplicable? Was the experience transformative, with reality now turned numinous and specter-laden, inhabited by wonder and amazement? Or had something like Weber's routine simply reasserted itself through strength of numbers, the weight of the everyday, apparitionless, world? As if we're not fit company for charisma after all. And music, the poem's other presence, what's the impact, the afterlife there? The meaning of our experience exceeds us, the poem seems to be saying, no matter how revelatory that experience may seem. We're all in the dark, left to guesswork."

KATHLEEN GRABER was born in Cape May County, New Jersey, in 1959. She teaches at Virginia Commonwealth University, and she divides her time between Richmond, Virginia, and her hometown of Wildwood, New Jersey, where for twenty-five years she and her husband operated a music shop on the Boardwalk. She is the author of two books of poetry, *Correspondence* (Saturnalia Books, 2005) and *The Eternal City* (Princeton University Press, 2010).

Of "Self-Portrait with No Internal Navigation," Graber writes: "When I travel back home to South Jersey from Virginia, I drive almost directly northeast so that I end up in Lewes, Delaware. A ferry runs between Cape Henlopen and Cape May. The journey across the Delaware Bay takes about eighty-five minutes, and because I often travel with my big dog, I usually sit in my car to keep him company and to read in the rocking silence. It didn't take long before I noticed the pigeons nesting on the pipes over my head. Unlike many people, I've always found pigeons remarkably beautiful and interesting. Not long before I wrote this poem, I had a strange dream that I was sleeping on a tightrope. I could speculate a lot about the meaning of that, but the immediate result was that I finally made the time to watch *Man on Wire,* the documentary about Philippe Petit and his walk between the twin towers of the World Trade Center. I have a great fear of heights (though I was not frightened in my dream!). I visited the World Trade Center only once—around 1980. I was a college student, and a friend who had come to NY to visit me wanted to do the sort of things tourists do. I could not even exit the elevator when its doors opened onto the observation deck of floor-to-ceiling glass. There are many things that lose some of their mystery when we dwell deeply upon them, but the idea that Philippe Petit walked between those buildings only becomes more and more astonishing to me the longer I consider it. And that particular feat has now been freighted by history with a unique poignancy. This poem was originally called 'Self-Portrait with Love Story,' but that seemed too sentimental to me."

AMY GLYNN GREACEN was born in the San Francisco Bay Area in 1972. She holds degrees from Mount Holyoke College and Lancaster University, England. She is a poet, a novelist, a food writer, an occasional essayist, and a contributing book reviewer for *The New York Quarterly*.

She has also moonlighted as a jazz vocalist since 1998. She lives outside San Francisco with her husband and two daughters.

Of *"Helianthus annuus* (Sunflower)," Greacen writes: "My ninth-grade algebra teacher was obsessed with the twelfth-century Italian mathematician Leonardo Fibonacci, and in particular the number sequence for which he is most famous, in which each number is the sum of the two numbers that precede it (0, 1, 1, 2, 3, 5, 8, 13, etc). I barely scraped a passing grade in that class, but later, her reverent mutterings about the golden mean and packing density and Fibonacci sequences dictating forms in nature began to come back to me. Fibonacci series occur, for instance, in the scales on pinecones and pineapples, the shell of the chambered nautilus, and perhaps most famously in the seed head of the sunflower. I was taken with the idea of the golden mean being represented by this golden flower, and with the fact that the mean is represented by the Greek letter ϕ, which if you squint at it you might see as an abstracted sunflower, a large disc on a straight stem. Being a bit of a nerd, I decided to see what would happen if I followed the Fibonacci sequence in my lines and discovered that it determined a certain pleasing packing density even on the page. (Mrs. G., if you're out there—I get it now!) The 'weary of time' reference comes from William Blake's poem 'Ah! Sunflower.' Contradicting Mr. Blake felt even more dangerous than passing notes in that algebra class, but with all due respect, it made more sense to me to see the sunflower as a supplicant to the sun god, Apollo, who is often associated with order and with the golden mean."

James Allen Hall was born in Columbus, Indiana, in 1976. His book of poems, *Now You're the Enemy* (University of Arkansas Press, 2008), won awards from the Lambda Literary Foundation, the Texas Institute of Letters, and the Fellowship of Southern Writers. He is the 2011 recipient of fellowships from the National Endowment for the Arts and the New York Foundation for the Arts. He teaches creative writing and literature at the State University of New York at Potsdam, in upstate New York.

Of "One Train's Survival Depends on the Other Derailed," Hall writes: "One night I was at a bar in Tucson called Plush, drinking whiskey with some poets. One young woman—not a poet, but flush with artistic air—told a story about her childhood pet, Bluebird, who was set free one evening from its cage by the babysitter, despite the child's prolonged pleas to keep the latch locked. The bird flew directly into an electrical socket and committed suicide. We were shocked, and not just because she'd prefaced Bluebird's tale with 'Here's a funny story.' The comedy existed in the prolonged pleas from the child, who was wise and wanted to keep her Bluebird alive. It seems she knew all along what the animal wanted.

"The next day, I drafted the poem. I'd been rereading poets I admire for their ability to pressurize story with lyric description and sonic texture, and went back to Susan Mitchell's *Rapture,* an important book in my development as a poet. I love—and borrowed—her maximalist sensibility, her use of the speaker's body as oracle, this choir-of-one who sings multiple experiences. The poem tries out her leaping connections, dizzyingly spun, so that the voice is changed by what it sings."

TERRANCE HAYES was born in Columbia, South Carolina, in 1971. He won the 2010 National Book Award in poetry for his book *Lighthead* (Penguin). His other books are *Wind in a Box* (Penguin, 2006), *Muscular Music* (Carnegie Mellon University Press, 2005), and *Hip Logic* (Penguin, 2002). His other honors include a Whiting Writers' Award, a National Endowment for the Arts Fellowship, a USA Zell Fellowship, and a Guggenheim Fellowship. He is a professor of creative writing at Carnegie Mellon University and lives in Pittsburgh, Pennsylvania.

Hayes writes: " 'The Rose Has Teeth' takes its title from the brilliant 2006 Matmos album, *The Rose Has Teeth in the Mouth of a Beast*—which takes its title from a passage in Ludwig Wittgenstein's *Philosophical Investigations.* 'Most artists are converted to art by art itself,' Lewis Hyde says in *The Gift.* My poem found its bones after I read Matthew Zapruder's marvelous poem 'Never to Return,' in the 2009 edition of *The Best American Poetry.* My poem found its breath at the piano I have been trying to play since 1999, the year my daughter was born."

STEVEN HEIGHTON is a poet, novelist, short story writer, and translator. He has received four gold National Magazine Awards in Canada, where he lives. His novel *Afterlands* (Houghton Mifflin, 2007) was published in six countries and has been optioned for film. His poetry collections are *Patient Frame* (House of Anansi Press, 2010), which includes the poem chosen for this year's *Best American Poetry, The Address Book* (House of Anansi Press, 2005), and *The Ecstasy of Skeptics* (House of Anansi Press, 1994). He has a website: www.stevenheighton.com.

Of "Collision," Heighton writes: "Kneeling next to a large doe as she lies dying beside a highway at two in the morning, after you've run into her with your car, is an experience most people would prefer to forget. I would prefer to forget it myself, but in my capacity as professional melancholic I've kept compulsively returning to the crash and its aftermath, trying for over a decade to make poetic sense of it.

"A number of tentative, groping first drafts went nowhere. Then, a few years ago, while reading Les Murray's volume of selected poems *Learning Human,* I discovered his remarkable 'The Cows on Killing Day.' In this poem the author, son of a dairy farmer, attempts to render a bovine perspective on . . . well, the title says it vividly enough. Murray's speculative ventriloquism led me to re-broach my own experience and try inverting the perspective from human to nonhuman. 'Collision' is the result.

"To some, the idea of writing seriously—as opposed to comically, mythically, allegorically, or in story-book fashion—from a nonhuman point of view might seem fatuous, if not slightly deranged. To me it seems a natural extension of the imaginative writer's staple project: that of trying to inhabit with sympathy the solitude of another being."

BRENDA HILLMAN is the author of eight collections of poetry, all published by Wesleyan University Press, the most recent of which are *Cascadia* (2001) and *Pieces of Air in the Epic* (2005), which received the William Carlos Williams Prize for Poetry, and *Practical Water* (2009). With Patricia Dienstfrey, she edited *The Grand Permission: New Writings on Poetics and Motherhood* (Wesleyan University Press, 2003). Hillman teaches at St. Mary's College in Moraga, California, where she is Olivia Filippi Professor of Poetry.

Of "Moaning Action at the Gas Pump," Hillman writes: "Poets and others can engage their powerful imaginations both in their writing and in direct action protests. These actions can be ceaselessly inventive, since authority knows how to respond to predictable behaviors, but the unpredictable cannot be tamed. Since the BP disaster, the oil companies have posted the largest profits in history. Not only must we cut our use of gas and find alternative energy, but surely we can also invent more anarchic protest actions against the destructive extraction of petroleum—actions that include discomfort and embarrassment outdoors. I decided it is a good form of street theater to moan audibly when pumping gas; tonally anarchic, the action is funny but includes tragedy and horror. I chose a prose-poem form because it conveys the feeling of an irreverent political tract. At the urging of Laura Mullen, I included some lines from a previous poem written after the first Gulf

War, 'Cheap Gas' (from *Loose Sugar*, Wesleyan University Press, 1997), as well as a transcription of the vowel-moan itself.

"At the time I was writing and revising the poem, I was engaged with several poets—Nick Flynn, Dorianne Laux, Fred Marchant, Laura Mullen, and Patricia Smith—in a dialogue about the tragedy for the magazine *Gulf Coast*. The epigraph comes from a beautiful essay by Nicole Loraux from *The Mourning Voice: An Essay on Greek Tragedy*, in which she notes that open mourning was prohibited for a while in ancient Greece because it was regarded as threatening. Jonathan Skinner reprinted the piece in *Interim* as part of his eco-activism issue; he encouraged poets to visit their representatives to protest offshore drilling."

JANE HIRSHFIELD was born in New York City in 1953 and has lived in Northern California since 1974. Her seventh and most recent book of poetry is *Come, Thief* (Alfred A. Knopf, 2011). *The Heart of Haiku* (Amazon Kindle Single, 2011) is an introduction to Bashō and haiku. Earlier books include *After* (HarperCollins, 2006) and *Given Sugar, Given Salt* (HarperCollins, 2001). She is the author of a book of essays, *Nine Gates: Entering the Mind of Poetry* (HarperCollins, 1997) and four books collecting and co-translating the work of poets from the past. She has won fellowships from the Guggenheim and Rockefeller Foundations, the National Endowment for the Arts, and the Academy of American Poets. In 2012, she was elected a Chancellor of the Academy and given the third annual Donald Hall–Jane Kenyon Poetry Award. This is her seventh appearance in *The Best American Poetry*.

Of "In a Kitchen Where Mushrooms Were Washed," Hirshfield writes: "I am interested in wick and fuel. Jane Brox's nonfiction book *Brilliant: The Evolution of Artificial Light* holds a description of early torches as irresistible to my jackdaw muse as a list of the Chinese names for jade once gathered from a dentist office's *National Geographic* or the painters' term *bonnarding*, learned from a friend. Each of these windfall images was mentally pocketed, held for some certain but unknowable future poem.

"There are times when something noticed provokes writing at once. So it was when I walked into a kitchen unmistakably fragrant. The mushrooms were gone—found, cleaned, carried elsewhere by a friend. The friend was gone, too. But I knew with surety something about the invisible past, and this raised in me a happiness somewhere between that of a truffle pig and Agatha Christie's Miss Marple.

"The poem started by this perception drew into itself the implausible sources for lamplight. Wild-found mushrooms are the opposite of torches: subterranean, secretive, damp. Shy of surface, their sense-realm is not the visual. Yet like any who traffic in the realms of existence and propagation, of eating and being eaten, they make themselves known—in this instance, by scent. I have long loved D. W. Winnicott's description of childhood: 'It is a joy to be hidden, but a disaster not to be found.' This poem began in outer facts, events, and observation, but its doorknob is to be found in the third stanza."

RICHARD HOWARD was born in Cleveland, Ohio, in 1929. He teaches in the writing division of Columbia University's School of the Arts, and continues against all odds to translate works of literature from the French. The most recent of his fifteen books of poems, *Without Saying*, was published in 2008 by Turtle Point Press. He was the guest editor of *The Best American Poetry 1995.* "A Proposed Curriculum Change" will be published by Turtle Point Press in his forthcoming book, *Progressive Education.* "Arthur Englander's Back in School," an earlier poem in the sequence, appeared in *The Best American Poetry 2009.*

Of "A Proposed Curriculum Change," Howard writes: "*Progressive Education* is a series of communications from the twelve members of the fifth-grade class of Park School in Sandusky, Ohio. In this case, the communication is a letter to the school principal, Mrs. Masters. The students at Park School, even or perhaps particularly those in the fifth-grade, are evidently proud of their vocabulary and their mastery of grown-up English."

MARIE HOWE was born in Rochester, New York, in 1950. Her books of poetry are *The Good Thief* (Persea Books, 1988), *What the Living Do* (W. W. Norton, 1997), and *The Kingdom of Ordinary Time* (W. W. Norton, 2008). She has taught at Sarah Lawrence College, Columbia, and New York University. She lives in New York City.

Of "Magdalene—The Seven Devils," Howe writes: "It occurred to me, walking through the city one day, that Mary Magdalene, who has been so often depicted and characterized by men, was a woman bedeviled—and then a woman clarified, integrated. What might have been the seven devils she was said to have been possessed by? And then, what are the devils we are possessed by? Then the poem began to speak."

AMORAK HUEY was born in Kalamazoo, Michigan, in 1969, and grew up outside Birmingham, Alabama. A decade ago he wound up back in Michigan, where he lives with his wife and two children. He spent fifteen years as a reporter and editor before leaving the newspaper business in 2008. He is now an assistant professor at Grand Valley State University, teaching creative and professional writing. His poems have appeared in numerous literary journals, and he blogs at his website, www.amorakhuey.net.

Of "Memphis," Huey writes: "I have been working on a collection of poems about blues music and musicians, about the South, about rivers. When I visited Memphis, all of those themes collided in one place. The whole place felt like a crossroads. The ghazal form seemed a great way to explore my fascination with this city. This poem is about longing, and temporariness, and being a tourist: the sense that we never entirely belong to any place or time. At least, I hope it's about those things. And music. Always music."

JENNY JOHNSON was born in Winchester, Virginia, in 1979. After earning a master of teaching degree from the University of Virginia, she taught public school for several years in the Bay Area. She then earned her MFA from Warren Wilson College. Currently, she is a visiting lecturer at the University of Pittsburgh.

Of "Aria," Johnson writes: "As a record collector and a fan of all sorts of music, I love thinking about the relationships between sounds and bodies. One way to think about 'Aria' is as seven meditations on this theme. In the opening sections, I was thinking about the music that arises out of the body. I also thought about plural pronouns, the turn toward a 'you,' the use of 'we' to capture what theorist Ann Cvetkovich calls 'public feelings.' When I refer to 'dance interludes' in sections 6 and 7, I am interested in music's ability to rattle bodies in public spaces, too. Specifically, I drew inspiration from Cvetkovich's *An Archive of Feelings: Trauma, Sexuality, and Lesbian Public Cultures,* a book that opens with a personal experience of a Le Tigre concert, a space where Cvetkovich felt a vital queer and lesbian subculture had formed in response to trauma. Having seen this band live, I knew what she meant and tried to write into this sensation.

"I also decided while working on 'Aria' that metrically I did not want to prioritize unity over disjunction. Rather, what I was most interested in was playing with the sounds and restraints that emerge from a queer body, the sounds that emerge from a queer collective, a body or voice that has the potential to be unified by its disjunctions."

LAWRENCE JOSEPH was born in Detroit, Michigan, in 1948. He attended the University of Michigan, the University of Cambridge, and the University of Michigan Law School. He is the author of five books of poetry: *Into It* (Farrar, Straus and Giroux, 2005), *Codes, Precepts, Biases, and Taboos: Poems 1973–1993* (Farrar, Straus and Giroux, 2005), *Before Our Eyes* (Farrar, Straus and Giroux, 1993), *Curriculum Vitae* (University of Pittsburgh Press, 1988), and *Shouting at No One* (University of Pittsburgh Press, 1983), which received the Agnes Lynch Starrett Poetry Prize. He has also written *Lawyerland* (Farrar, Straus and Giroux, 1997), a book of prose, and *The Game Changed: Essays and Other Prose* (University of Michigan Press, 2011). He is Tinnelly Professor of Law at St. John's University School of Law, where he teaches courses on labor, employment, tort and compensation law, legal theory, jurisprudence, and law and interpretation. He has won a fellowship from the Guggenheim Foundation and has taught creative writing at Princeton University. Married to the painter Nancy Van Goethem, he lives in downtown Manhattan.

Joseph writes: "There's a couplet in the opening poem of Wallace Stevens's last book of poems, *The Rock*: 'The self and the earth—your thoughts, your feelings, / Your beliefs and disbeliefs, your whole peculiar plot.' The whole of my work is my 'whole peculiar plot.' I see myself—as Stevens and as Eugenio Montale and Louis Zukofsky did—writing, plotting, one long poem.

"'So Where Are We?' is the title poem of my next book. My last book, *Into It,* contains poems, or parts of poems, which touch on the 9/11 World Trade Center attacks. My reaction to the terrorist bombings has an intensely personal dimension. My wife and I live a block from Ground Zero. Shortly before the first plane hit on the morning of September 11, I left her to go to St. John's University in Queens, where I teach. Nancy spent that night in our apartment. More than twenty-four hours went by before I saw her again. We were evacuated from our apartment for over two months.

"Before I write a poem, I usually try to imagine the form or shape it will take. I feel the form or shape visually ('conversation as design' was one of William Carlos Williams's definitions of poetry). Then, in effect, I load the shape or form with parts of the entire world of my subjects—with my 'whole peculiar plot.' I imagined 'So Where Are We?' in couplets. I also envisaged it as the second part of a diptych, the first part being 'Unyieldingly Present,' a poem in couplets in *Into It* written as a compressed, collective portrayal of the terrorist attacks."

FADY JOUDAH was born in Austin, Texas, in 1971. Married with two kids, he is a practicing physician of internal medicine in Houston, Texas. *The Earth in the Attic,* his first poetry collection, was selected by Louise Glück for the Yale Series of Younger Poets in 2008. His two translations of Mahmoud Darwish's poetry (from Copper Canyon in 2007 and Farrar, Straus and Giroux in 2010) received a TLS/Banipal prize from the United Kingdom and a PEN USA award for translation, respectively. His second book, *Alight,* is due from Copper Canyon Press in 2013. And his most recent translation of Palestinian poet Ghassan Zaqtan, *Like a Straw Bird It Follows Me,* is available this year from Yale University Press.

Of "Tenor," Joudah writes: "In George Oppen's 'Semite' these lines always haunt me: 'Think // think also of the children / the guards laughing // the one pride the pride / of the warrior laughing so the hangman / comes to all dinners.' To say that I had the children of Gaza in mind when I wrote 'Tenor' would be as accurate as saying Oppen had only one child in mind in his poem. War not only kills children, any children, but also destroys childhood, all childhood."

JOY KATZ was born in Newark, New Jersey, two months before John F. Kennedy was shot. Her latest collection, *All You Do Is Perceive,* is due in 2013 from Four Way Books. She teaches in the graduate writing program at Chatham University and at the University of Pittsburgh and lives in Pittsburgh with her husband and young son.

Of "Death Is Something Entirely Else," Katz writes: "When my son—now nearly five—was a baby, I spent all of my waking hours either feeling stoned or imagining my own death. The trance state was due partly to oxytocin, a natural hormone released during breast-feeding. I wasn't breast-feeding; I'm an adoptive mom, so that caring-for-baby chemistry (it feels like a heroin high) was a nice bonus. As for imagining my death—I guess most new parents do. I never felt so mortal.

"I tried for a long time to record the feeling of being with the baby in those hours when he was engaged in some activity (as in this poem: dropping sheets of printer paper onto my face) and not paying too much attention to me. This is one of those attempts. The feelings I experienced were terrifying and rapturous. Simply the act of regarding him was joy, and a cliff-edge mortality was part of that joy."

JAMES KIMBRELL was born in Jackson, Mississippi, in 1967. He is the author of two volumes of poetry, *The Gatehouse Heaven* (1998) and *My*

Psychic (2006), both from Sarabande Books. He has won a Whiting Award, a Ruth Lilly Fellowship, and a fellowship from the National Endowment for the Arts. He recently served as the Renée and John Grisham Writer in Residence at the University of Mississippi. He taught at Westminster (Missouri) and Kenyon Colleges before moving to Tallahassee, Florida, where he is an associate professor of English at Florida State University.

Of "How to Tie a Knot," Kimbrell writes: "I wanted to ground this poem in a physical hunger that might give voice to a more or less spiritual desire, the desire for access to the real, whatever it might finally be. In this pursuit, a variation on a line from Robert Duncan's gorgeous 'In the South' makes an appearance, but mostly what we have here are the musings of someone acting out a self-inflicted deserted island scenario in which half the day is spent trying to make sense of the conflicting desires that govern our days, while the other half is spent losing bait. Amen."

NOELLE KOCOT was born in Brooklyn, New York, in 1969. She lives in New Jersey and teaches writing in New York City. She is the author of five books of poetry, *4* (Four Way Books, 2001), *The Raving Fortune* (Four Way Books, 2004), *Poem for the End of Time and Other Poems* (Wave Books, 2006), *Sunny Wednesday* (Wave Books, 2009), and *The Bigger World* (Wave Books, 2011). She is also the author of a discography, *Damon's Room* (Wave Books, 2010), and she translated some of the poems of Tristan Corbière from the French, which are collected in a book called *Poet by Default* (Wave Books, 2011). She is the widow of composer Damon Tomblin, who died in 2004, "and left me speechless. I write poems every day just to get away from the grief and sadness I experience without him being on the earth anymore. But still, I have a lot going on in my life, and am pretty happy when the day is done."

MAXINE KUMIN was born in Germantown (Philadelphia), Pennsylvania, in 1925. Her seventeenth poetry collection, *Where I Live: New & Selected Poems 1990–2010,* published by W. W. Norton, received the *Los Angeles Times* Book Award for 2011. A former United States Poet Laureate and winner of the Pulitzer and Ruth Lilly Poetry Prizes, she lives with her husband on a farm in New Hampshire. A retired professor, she is "now content to be a writer and poet."

Of "Either Or," Kumin writes: "I've paraphrased the late astronomer Loren Eisley, and somewhere I read the famous quotation from

Socrates. These sorts of fragments tend to adhere; sometimes they lead to poems. The rest describes exactly how it is where we live."

SARAH LINDSAY was born in Cedar Rapids, Iowa, in 1958. A Paracollege graduate of St. Olaf College, she holds an MFA from the University of North Carolina, Greensboro. Her books are *Primate Behavior* (Grove Press, 1997), *Mount Clutter* (Grove Press, 2002), and *Twigs and Knuckle-bones* (Copper Canyon Press, 2008). She plays the cello with a regularly nonperforming group and has worked for more than twenty years as a copy editor for Pace Communications in Greensboro, where she lives with her spouse.

Of "Hollow Boom Soft Chime: The Thai Elephant Orchestra," Lindsay writes: "For domesticated Asian elephants, it's hard to find gainful employment. In preserves that save their lives and give them space and water to bathe in, some have been taught to paint, and some made recordings as the Thai Elephant Orchestra. The instruments modified for elephants are mostly percussive—bells, gongs, drums—but the harmonica works well, too, and the occasional vocal ad lib. Given the apparatus, the players' thumps and jangles and gongs are not exactly instinctive behavior, but they follow an elephant's sense of the beat and the tone, not ours; and every 'piece' has an unresolved other-ness like whale song."

AMIT MAJMUDAR was born in New York City in 1979. Having earned his MD in 2003, he works as a diagnostic nuclear radiologist in Dublin, Ohio. His books of poetry are *0°, 0°* (TriQuarterly/Northwestern University Press, 2009) and *Heaven and Earth* (Story Line Press), which received the 2011 Donald Justice Award. His novels are *Partitions* (Holt/Metropolitan, 2011) and *The Abundance* (forthcoming from Holt/Metropolitan).

Of "The Autobiography of Khwaja Mustasim," Majmudar writes: "Khwaja Mustasim is an elderly Afghan schoolteacher, Mustasim Mujahid Rahman. He currently lives in Herat, which Word's spell-check function insists on switching to 'Heart.' Mustasim's (Sufi Muslim) name happens to be an uncanny near-rearrangement of my own (Hindu) full name, Amit Himanshu Majmudar. (The extra 's' is the serpent in the garden.) Mustasim likes to joke about this anagram-matical connection between us—he calls me his 'infidel amanuensis.' I call him my 'dapple-dawn-drawn doppelganger.' We are good friends, Mustasim and I.

"Khwaja Mustasim dictated his 'Autobiography' to me in a form derived either from the Holy Qur'an or the Book of Taliesin. To this day I am uncertain which. I notice that he tells his life *as a series of past lives,* though he does not, as a Muslim, believe in rebirth—while *I,* as a Hindu, do. Might this 'Autobiography' be a kind of metaphysical joke? And if so, at whose expense?

"I tried to pin old Mustasim down on this question, and he explained to me (in Sanskrit, no less) that a man of faith embodies his faith—and the whole history of his faith. 'So when anyone, martyr or murderer, speaks Islam, he speaks me,' said Mustasim. 'I figured I should fight back like your long-lined poet Whitman: By singing myself.'"

DAVID MASON was born in Bellingham, Washington, in 1954. He is professor of English and creative writing at the Colorado College, and he serves as poet laureate of Colorado. A critic and opera librettist as well as a poet, Mason has written words for Lori Laitman's oratorio, *Vedem,* which is now out on CD from Naxos, and also for her opera *The Scarlet Letter,* which will have its professional premiere at Opera Colorado in May 2013. Mason's most recent books are *The Scarlet Libretto* (Red Hen Press, 2012), *Two Minds of a Western Poet* (essays; University of Michigan Press, 2011), and a memoir, *News from the Village* (Red Hen Press, 2010). He has edited a number of anthologies, including *Twentieth-Century American Poetry* (with Dana Gioia and Meg Schoerke; McGraw-Hill, 2003) and *Contemporary American Poems* for the General Administration for Press and Publication of the People's Republic of China (GAPP), 2011, a project of the National Endowment for the Arts.

Of "Mrs. Mason and the Poets," Mason writes: "There's something wonderful about being out of date, and also about reading books that are no longer current. When by chance I found Edmund Blunden's biography of Percy Bysshe Shelley at Henderson Books in my home town of Bellingham, Washington, I immediately thought two things: I don't know much about Shelley, and I know next to nothing about Blunden. I bought the book and devoured it. Blunden wrote with eccentric panache and the sympathetic authority of a real poet. Rather than trying to be exhaustive, he elucidated only the stuff that really interested him.

"When I stumbled on a few details about Lady Mount Cashell, the Irish aristocrat living in sin with a Mr. Tighe, and learned they had assumed the name Mason to protect themselves against scandal at home, I knew at once I would write something about them. I did not know I would adopt Mrs. Mason's voice. Nor did I know I would make use of Shelley's death by drowning in the poem, though dying young is a theme that has often arrested my attention.

"As for the rest, it's all imagination and empathy."

KERRIN MCCADDEN was born in Lexington, Massachusetts, in 1966. She teaches English and creative writing at Montpelier High School and poetry at the New England Young Writers' Conference at Bread Loaf. She lives in Plainfield, Vermont.

Of "Becca," McCadden writes: "I like collisions. I like to bang things together inside a poem and use a tangle of rubber bands to hold it together. In this poem, there is a clear story, and, I believe, a clear understory, but there are also a pile of antique bird books, Kafka, geography, my standing love of etymology and fonts, Mary Oliver, and the terror and thrill of letting children go. There is something in the gathering storm of wide and disparate reading that charges me for writing. I am fond of a coming-of-age poem that leans on Kafka, of a wish for a beautiful life that leans on tattooing, of a man who creates beauty all day by inking people's skin but does not know what a stanza is—who thinks it's a kind of bird.

"This poem is also an homage to a young poet whom I admire, Becca Starr. I bet she will outwrite me. Let this little paragraph be a gauntlet on the floor."

HONOR MOORE was born in 1945 in New York City, where she returned to live in September 2011, after years in the countryside of northwestern Connecticut. She is the author of three collections of poems: *Red Shoes* (W. W. Norton, 2005), *Darling* (Grove Press, 2001), and *Memoir* (Chicory Blue Press, 1988). She has also written *The White Blackbird: A Life of the Painter Margarett Sargent by Her Granddaughter* (Viking, 1996) and *The Bishop's Daughter* (W. W. Norton, 2008), a memoir. She has edited *Poems from the Women's Movement* (Library of America, 2009), *The New Women's Theatre* (Vintage Books, 1977), and *Amy Lowell: Selected Poems* (Library of America, 2004). She is on the graduate writing faculty at the New School and was recently Distinguished Visiting Writer at the University of Richmond (2011) and the University of Iowa (2010 and 2012).

Moore writes: " 'Song' began as many pages (yellow legal pad, handwritten in blue ink and pencil) that came late one Sunday afternoon when I allowed myself to imagine freely a night of lovemaking with the proviso that I use the physical world to render my delight and desire. I never throw away a draft, and this one, over years of revision, took no form, getting shorter and shorter as time went on. Finally, I thought, why don't you try to make it a sonnet? And so it has ended up as an eccentrically tetrameter example of that daunting form. I hoped the title might encourage readers to take the poem on its simple, almost fairy-tale terms, entering its music, indulging its alliteration."

MICHAEL MORSE was born in New York City in 1966, grew up in Roslyn, New York, and attended Oberlin College and the University of Iowa. He lives in Brooklyn, New York, and teaches at the Ethical Culture Fieldston School, the Iowa Summer Writing Festival, and the Gotham Writers' Workshop.

Of "Void and Compensation (Facebook)," Morse writes: "A few years ago, within the span of a month, a number of my high-school classmates and I started to communicate again via Facebook. There they were, after twenty-five years of no contact, posting updates and pictures on a 'wall.' They were familiar yet different—some with families, some with different names, all of them magically narrowing a generation's worth of time in two or three minutes. For anyone living in New York during 9/11, a 'wall' with words and photos has a haunting resonance. The poem emerged from contemplating a wall for the no-longer-missing (and their uncanny, sudden resurfacings) and remembering a wall for those still missing. I was thinking about friends no longer living, friends with whom I wish I were still in touch. In particular I miss Leo Millar, a college friend, and this poem is an elegy for him."

CAROL MUSKE-DUKES was born in St. Paul, Minnesota, in 1945. She is a professor at the University of Southern California and has also taught at Columbia, the Iowa Writers' Workshop, the University of Virginia, and the University of California, Irvine. She is the author of eight books of poetry, four novels, and two essay collections. Her most recent books are *Twin Cities* (Penguin, 2011) and two anthologies: *Crossing State Lines: An American Renga,* coedited with Bob Holman (Farrar, Straus and Giroux, 2011) and *The Magical Poetry Blimp Pilot's Guide,* coedited with Diana Arterian (Figueroa Press, 2011). Her other books of poetry include *Sparrow* (Random House, 2003), *An Octave Above Thunder, New and Selected Poems* (Penguin, 1997), and *Red Trousseau* (Viking/Penguin, 1991). Her collection of reviews and critical essays, *Women and Poetry:*

Truth, Autobiography, and the Shape of the Self, was published in the "Poets on Poetry" series of the University of Michigan Press in 1997. She has received a Guggenheim Fellowship, a National Endowment for the Arts Fellowship, an Ingram-Merrill Foundation Award, the Witter Bynner award from the Library of Congress, and the Castagnola Award from the Poetry Society of America. For many years she was poetry columnist for the *Los Angeles Times Book Review.* On November 13, 2008, Governor Schwarzenegger appointed Carol as California's poet laureate.

Of "Hate Mail," Muske-Dukes writes: "I am (and have always been) an outspoken woman. Thus I've acquired a lot of friends and also a few enemies. Someone in the latter group began sending me anonymous 'hate' email not long ago. If you have ever received hate mail, you know that it is quite scary—especially if the unknown correspondent has 'facts' about your life, and appears to have some familiarity with your day-to-day life and your family and friends. The emails I received were somewhat threatening, but they were mostly just rantings by an odd, not-very-intelligent, very angry person who did not like me at all. (My webmaster and others tried to track the emails, but the author had disappeared into cyberspace, impossible to trace.)

"At one point, I realized that this mail was kind of funny. The ability to reread the emails and laugh at them gave me the idea of writing a parody: writing hate mail to myself. Of course, the bizarre insulting perspective and nutzoid observations of my poem are original, are mine—but the 'spirit' of the disturbed correspondent inspired my 'voice' in the poem.

"Goethe said, 'A poet must know how to hate.' I've always written poems of love and loss. I must say that I found it absolutely exhilarating to write a 'hate' poem, especially a hate poem to myself. It was cathartic, but it was also kind of inspiring—I think I may have a talent for this! I experienced the 'freeing' of a reckless voice, the freedom of (faux) anonymity. Perhaps I'll crank out a couple more."

ANGELO NIKOLOPOULOS was born in Los Angeles, California, in 1981. He is a graduate of New York University's Creative Writing Program. His first book of poems, *Obscenely Yours,* won the Kinereth Gensler Award and is forthcoming from Alice James Books. He teaches creative writing at Rutgers University, New Brunswick, and hosts the White Swallow Reading Series in New York City.

Nikolopoulos writes: "Like most of my poems, 'Daffodil' emerged out of a briny mixture of self-contempt and nostalgia. I was thinking of my early twenties—an unapologetic time for most of the gay men I knew—and how I wore my sex on my sleeve like a garish motel sign: *Vacancy, always.*

"San Francisco, 2002: I was blond-streaked and *giving it* and obnoxious, like Wordsworth's daffodils. But aren't all such lavish displays a performance, an act of covering up? (Stale Nag Champa burns in the dormitory.) The poem's more Gerard Manley Hopkins then—'A little sickness in the air / From too much fragrance everywhere:'—since spring's a prelude to death after all.

"So I wanted to write a poem about youth that both admired and despised it at the same time. It's a song of praise and condemnation then—both *Hello, how've you been?* and, thankfully, *Good riddance.*"

MARY OLIVER was born in the Cleveland suburb of Maple Heights in 1935. She attended both Ohio State University and Vassar College, though she did not receive a degree. Her first collection of poems, *No Voyage, and Other Poems,* was published in 1963 by Dent Press in the United Kingdom. She has since published fifteen books of poetry and five books of prose. *American Primitive* (Little, Brown, 1983) received the Pulitzer Prize in 1984, and *New and Selected Poems* (Beacon Press, 1992) won the National Book Award in 1992. The first part of her book-length poem *The Leaf and the Cloud* (Da Capo Press, 2000) was selected for inclusion in *The Best American Poetry 1999* and the second part, "Work," was selected for *The Best American Poetry 2000.* Her books of prose include *Long Life: Essays and Other Writings* (Da Capo Press, 2004). Beacon Press published *New and Selected Poems, Volume Two* in 2005 as well as her first poetry CD, *At Blackwater Pond,* in 2006. *Red Bird* was published by Beacon Press in 2008. Mary Oliver held the Catharine Osgood Foster Chair for Distinguished Teaching at Bennington College until 2001. She has lived in Provincetown, Massachusetts, for more than forty years.

Of "In Provincetown, and Ohio, and Alabama," Oliver writes: "The poem follows my usual path. I go out into the world and look and reflect, listen and consider. A great deal of what I find, and more and more lately, is simply action and noise. The world is changing, as it always has and always will. But something is missing in all that activity; the way we use the earth is like a victor's use after the last battle. And yet everything is part of a mystery—*the* mystery—and therein, so I believe, is a holiness. So I didn't pass the mule in haste but considered the flowers coming from its body, gave it at least a few moments of deep attention, and, with the last adjective, placed it within that mysterious (and holy) territory."

STEVE ORLEN was born in Holyoke, Massachusetts, in 1942. He taught poetry craft in the MFA program of the University of Arizona for more than thirty years, shepherding dozens of young poets into bright careers, including Michael Collier, Richard Siken, David Wojahn, and Tony Hoagland. He received NEA grants and a Guggenheim Fellowship, and published many books, including *The Elephant's Child: New & Selected Poems, 1978–2005* (Ausable Press, 2006). He died in November 2010. A month before his death he reported to the editors of *New Ohio Review,* where "Where Do We Go After We Die" would posthumously appear, that "The weather is cooler, my back & my hip joint flagellate me with every step, my wife is lovely, our son and his wife are visiting from LA and we told them all we want to do is stare at them and hug every once in a while, and Tony and Kath—I think you're friends with them?—are off soon for Majorca, where they're hoping to be included on a dig for the soul of Robert Graves."

Tony Hoagland, Steve Orlen's literary executor, writes: "Steve wrote under the constellation of Randall Jarrell, the wisest of his own generation of poets, and 'Where Do We Go After We Die' is a fine example of that wise, tender mode, braiding fable, anecdote, and meditation upon an undertone of philosophical acceptance. The Jon in the poem is the poet Jon Anderson, Steve's lifelong friend. As young poets, they labeled themselves 'Sincerists,' and sought to write poems modeled upon perfect conversation between intimates, embodying 'the poignant bravery of the living.' What's spectacular in 'Where Do We Go After We Die' are the many nuanced fluencies of texture and intelligence, and the masterly closing movement, in which 'speech reverts' from the personal to a more omniscient perspective: 'And actions lose their agency—*It came to pass*—' The poem is about stories as much as death: its final lines rather magically depict the end of all the narratives, and the onset of speechlessness."

ALICIA OSTRIKER was born in 1937 in New York City and hopes to return there after living most of her life in Princeton, New Jersey. She has published fourteen volumes of poetry, most recently *No Heaven* (2007), *The Book of Seventy* (2009), and *The Book of Life: Selected Jewish Poems, 1979–2011* (2012), all with the University of Pittsburgh Press. She has also written several books of critical essays on poetry and on the

Bible, most recently *For the Love of God: The Bible as an Open Book* (Rutgers University Press, 2007). She teaches in the low-residency program at Drew University.

Ostriker writes: " 'Song' is one of a series of poems spoken by the old woman, the tulip, and the dog. They have come as a relief after a period of working on a series of poems of heavy self-examination and spiritual quest. I suppose they, too, may be a species of self-examination, but they continue to surprise me. Most people seem to like the dog best, but I am fond of all three characters."

ERIC PANKEY was born in Kansas City, Missouri, in 1959. Educated in the public school system, he completed his undergraduate work in 1981 at the University of Missouri, Columbia, and earned his MFA in 1983 at the University of Iowa. He is the author of eight collections of poems. His first, *For the New Year* (Atheneum, 1984), won the Walt Whitman Award. *Heartwood* came out from Atheneum in 1988 and was reissued by Orchises Press in 1998. His next three collections were published by Alfred A. Knopf: *Apocrypha* in 1991, *The Late Romances* in 1997, and *Cenotaph* in 2000. Ausable Press published *Oracle Figures* in 2003, *Reliquaries* in 2005, and *The Pear as One Example: New & Selected Poems 1984–2008* in 2008. New collections are forthcoming from Milkweed Editions. The recipient of fellowships from the National Endowment for the Arts, the Ingram Merrill Foundation, and the Guggenheim Foundation, he teaches at George Mason University, where he is professor of English and holds the Heritage Chair in writing.

Of "Sober Then Drunk Again," Pankey writes: "The title does the work of narration in this little lyric. Sober for many years, I tried my hand at drinking again, and apart from the consumption of many fine bottles of wine, little good came of my failed attempt to drink moderately. A melancholic to start with, I was pulled even deeper down by alcohol and the lead weight of depression. This is a poem voiced from that depth."

LUCIA PERILLO was born in New York City in 1958. *Inseminating the Elephant* (Copper Canyon Press, 2009), her fifth book of poems, received the Washington State Book Award and the Bobbitt Prize from the Library of Congress. In 2012 she published a book of stories, *Happiness Is a Chemical in the Brain,* along with a new book of poems, *On the Spectrum of Possible Deaths.*

Of "Samara," Perillo writes: "A *samara* is beautiful both as a word and as a thing. It is all but impossible to believe that the engineering of its perfect thingliness could have been accomplished by so random a process as natural selection—but this is just to restate the poem.

"I'm not much of a celebrator, but if I were going to start celebrating, the samara is probably the thing I'd start with. An ideal form, in such marvelous nonmotorized flight, which maybe, serendipitously, gets buried in the dirt, where instead of rotting it starts bursting toward the light as it becomes that complicated thing, a tree. A much better system than ours!—wherein our corpses don't grow, nourish nothing, and are too chemically infused even to rot.

"Though the readers and writers of poetry are a somewhat obscure subculture in our day and age, they (we) still have codes of conduct and attitude (like: thou shalt not be a warmongering Republican). There's also pressure—or this is just my imagination?—to keep on the sunny side of the street, or, as Roethke said, 'Praise to the end!' But where are the songs of our gory going-down-into-sludge? The cries of 'Oh, it's so unfair'? Or: 'Holy Fuck, somebody do something, the morphine's not working'? The calls for mortality to be replaced, and now—if we can put a man on the moon, surely we can do this, not to live forever, ugh, but to be recycled for some purpose? To come to a graceful end, which is also a beginning?"

ROBERT PINSKY was born in Long Branch, New Jersey, in 1940. His *Selected Poems* was published in paperback in March 2012 by Farrar, Straus and Giroux. His CD *PoemJazz,* with the pianist Laurence Hobgood, has been released by Circumstantial Productions. He has won the Italian *Premio Capri,* the Harold Washington Award from the City of Chicago, and the *Los Angeles Times* Book Prize for his translation of *The Inferno of Dante* (Farrar, Straus and Giroux, 1996). He served as poet laureate of the United States from 1997 until 2000. He is also the author of several critical books, such as *The Situation of Poetry* (Princeton University Press, 1977), an interactive fiction computer game (*Mindwheel,* 1984), and a prose book about King David, *The Life of David* (Shocken, 2006). He lives in Cambridge, Massachusetts, and teaches in the graduate writing program at Boston University.

Of "Improvisation on Yiddish," Pinsky writes: "I have no idea how to spell the few dozen Yiddish words and phrases I know. They are part of my heard and spoken language—which is to say, the quality of language that interests me as a poet.

"In that heard and spoken texture, Yiddish is not italicized: it is continuous with the English I have spoken and heard, not set off from it as though it were ancient Greek or Latin. 'Improvisation on Yiddish' reflects that fact."

DEAN RADER was born in Stockton, California, in 1967 and grew up in Weatherford, Oklahoma, a farm town along Route 66. His debut collection of poems, *Works & Days* (Truman State University Press, 2010), won the 2010 T. S. Eliot Prize. His most recent scholarly book, *Engaged Resistance: American Indian Art, Literature, and Film from Alcatraz to the NMAI,* was published in 2011 by the University of Texas Press. He is a professor at the University of San Francisco, where he recently received the university's Distinguished Research Award.

Rader writes: "One thing I try to do in my book *Works & Days* is pose questions about identity. I wrote a series of self-portraits that are less sketches of the self and more like episodes of selfhood enacted through dialogues. Some of the dialogues are serious; some are goofy. Among the least goofy is 'Self-Portrait as Dido to Aeneas.' Here I was interested in the connection between and among couplets, couple, and coupling. And I was thinking about how long poetic lines might some-how convey how long love (and loss) lasts. I also just like the character of Dido, and I wanted a version of the story in which she makes Aeneas doubt every future decision, she gets her say, and it is her words (not his deeds) we remember."

SPENCER REECE was born in Hartford, Connecticut, in 1963. An Episcopal priest currently serving as the chaplain to Bishop Carlos López-Lozano of the Reformed Episcopal Church of Spain, he lives in Madrid, Spain. His first book of poems, *The Clerk's Tale,* won the Bakeless Prize sponsored by Houghton Mifflin in 2003. Farrar, Straus and Giroux will publish his second book of poems, *The Road to Emmaus,* in 2013.

Reece writes: "The people who change our lives are often mysteries. We never really understand them. This seems to me the crux of the story in the Bible that comes at the end of the Gospel According to St. Luke, 'The Road to Emmaus.' The author of Luke may also have writ-ten Acts, the book that follows Luke in the Bible. The Emmaus story hinges Luke to Acts. The book of Acts shows how the faith spread. And so this story links the grief over death with the hope found in faith. The two disciples, Cleopas and the unnamed disciple, do not realize, at first, what is in front of them. This experience, of not realizing the love that is in front of you until it is gone, resonates deeply for me. Much of the work behind the poem came through the spiritual direction I received from an unassuming Catholic nun of the Franciscan order over a seven-year period. I wanted to pay tribute to nuns in this poem: they, too, are an expression of love before us that is disappearing."

PAISLEY REKDAL was born in Seattle, Washington, in 1970. She is the author of four books of poetry: *A Crash of Rhinos* (University of Georgia Press, 2000), *Six Girls Without Pants* (Eastern Washington University Press, 2002), *The Invention of the Kaleidoscope* (University of Pittsburgh Press, 2007), and *Animal Eye* (University of Pittsburgh Press, 2012). She has also written a book of essays, *The Night My Mother Met Bruce Lee* (Vintage Books, 2002), and a hybrid photo-text memoir entitled *Intimate* (Tupelo Books, 2012). She teaches at the University of Utah in Salt Lake City.

Of "Wax," Rekdal writes: "This poem took eight months to write. My inspiration was twofold: first, John Ashbery's 'Self-Portrait in a Convex Mirror,' which I play with a little bit here; second, the work of my friend Lela Graybill, an art historian at the University of Utah, who is at work on a book about the French Revolution and spectacles of violence. I thought at first that this poem, a response to her work, would be short: two pages at most. Then I started doing research about wax, and fell headlong into an obsession with it as a material medium. More pliable and far less durable than stone, used mainly for modeling processes rather than for finished products, what does a waxwork suggest about permanence? I was also fascinated—OK, maybe freaked out—by why we would feel the need to make a life-size representation of someone like, say, Charles Manson or Angelina Jolie out of a lump of congealed fatty acids, and then pay money to have our pictures taken with it. None of it made sense. Around the same time, as is evident in the poem, my mother had cancer—one of the latest in a string of people in my family who'd had some form of this disease—and suddenly my family and I were having lively, cocktail-fueled dinner conversations about things like genetic testing and end-of-life care. I never thought these issues were related until thirty dead pages into my second draft when I began to realize that my obsession with wax was perhaps an obsession with the ways we see ourselves and our loved ones when we are least in control of our bodies. Once I understood that, the poem began to come to life. The rest was—as it always is—subtraction."

MARY RUEFLE was born in McKeesport, Pennsylvania, in 1952. Her latest book is *Madness, Rack, and Honey* (Wave Books, 2012), a collection of lectures on poetry. Her *Selected Poems* (Wave Books) appeared in 2010. She has written a second book of prose, *The Most of It* (Wave Books, 2008). She is an artist who erases, treats, and extra-illustrates nineteenth-century books (maryruefle.com). She lives in Vermont.

Of "Middle School," Ruefle writes: "When I reread this poem, two lost memories return. Once I was watching an Italian film (whose name, sadly, I can't recall) and one of its scenes was shot in front of 'Cesare Pavese Middle School.' I loved that! It lodged in my mind long enough to appear in the poem. Another time I was in a Laundromat, staring at the floor. I found a wonderful object there, a little totem figure, a chieftain made entirely out of twist ties twisted together. I took this figure home and for a couple of years he sat on my desk until I gave him to a friend in need of such a thing. I would like to take this opportunity to divulge (now that no one cares) that my principal, in whose office I stood trembling many a time, was later arrested for shoplifting and lost his job. I imagine he must have fallen into a great depression, and come at last to understand those he shepherded. Let us hope."

DON RUSS was born in Wildwood, Florida, in 1943. He is a retired professor of literature, composition, and film now living and writing in Atlanta. He has published a volume of poems, *Dream Driving* (Kennesaw State University Press, 2007), and a chapbook, *Adam's Nap* (Billy Goat Press, 2005).

Russ writes: " 'Girl with Gerbil' began as an entry in a notebook: 'a constellation of air-holes punched into the lid of a shoebox—night sky for a little girl's gerbil.' The shoebox was temporary, and the little girl I knew is now a young woman. By the time I got back to it, the original idea had begun to gather into itself other preoccupations of mine. Little worlds—snow globes, doll houses, shadow boxes, and such—have fascinated me for my entire life, and now more than ever I wonder about this little world of ours lost in this very big and very mysterious universe."

KAY RYAN was born in California in 1945. She has published eight books of poetry, including *Flamingo Watching* (Copper Beech Press, 1994), and *Elephant Rocks* (1996), *Say Uncle* (2000), *The Niagara River* (2005), and *The Best of It: New and Selected Poems* (2010), all from Grove Press. *The Best of It* was awarded the Pulitzer Prize in 2011. She served as United States Poet Laureate from 2008 to 2010.

Of "Playacting," Ryan writes: "Reading W. G. Sebald one morning I came upon his reference to playacting, how tribal cultures kept hold of a sense that their rites weren't exactly real even though they might really die as a result of them. This sounded pretty much like life. I recognized the feeling of being a little abstracted. It's a problem, how to die inside something never quite convincingly real.

"No, actually, it's not a problem, in that it will happen whether I agree or not. But it is interesting—interesting to admit that one is not utterly convinced, to go ahead and admit it and to let one's mind move around from there. I find these thoughts quite horrible, but the mind doesn't care if thoughts are horrible; it's just so glad that they're interesting."

MARY JO SALTER was born in Grand Rapids, Michigan, in 1954. She is the author of six books of poems, all published by Alfred A. Knopf. The most recent is *A Phone Call to the Future: New and Selected Poems* (2008). She is also the editor of Amy Clampitt's *Selected Poems* (Alfred A. Knopf, 2010), and a coeditor of *The Norton Anthology of Poetry,* 4th and 5th editions. She lives in Baltimore, where she is Andrew W. Mellon Professor in the Humanities at the Writing Seminars of Johns Hopkins University.

Salter writes: "The setting of 'The Gods' is familiar to the poet: I often find myself in the cheapest seats in the concert hall. In the third or fourth balcony, one may feel far closer to the architect than to the composer, and the mind wanders. Who are the gods or goddesses pictured on the mural? Who chose John Greenleaf Whittier's name to be engraved in marble? Since I can't see the musicians very well, why don't I just close my eyes and listen?

"What surprised me as the poem unfolded is that it became, if not very polemically, a feminist poem. I hadn't expected that. Why aren't there any women's names inscribed inside the dome? Do I dare to slip into a seat closer to the action—say, seat D9, which I haven't paid for?

"'The Gods' has its political side, for sure. But I hope the poem is at least a little funny—that it acknowledges the timeless human comedy."

LYNNE SHARON SCHWARTZ was born in 1939 in Brooklyn, New York, a time and place she immortalized (well, sort of) in her 1989 novel, *Leaving Brooklyn* (Houghton Mifflin). She began writing poetry in childhood, but after that wrote mostly prose. However, now and then she is seized with the urge to return to poetry, and from those urges came her first collection, *In Solitary* (Sheep Meadow Press, 2002), and her most recent, *See You in the Dark* (Northwestern University Press, 2012).

Schwartz's twenty-two books include memoirs (*Ruined by Reading: A Life in Books,* Beacon Press, 1997) and story collections (*Acquainted with the Night,* Harper & Row, 1984). Her translations from Italian include *A Place to Live: And Other Selected Essays of Natalia Ginzburg,* and *Smoke over Birkenau,* by Liana Millu, which received the PEN Renato Poggioli Award for Translation. She has received grants from the Guggenheim Foundation, the National Endowment for the Arts, and the New York State Foundation for the Arts. She teaches at the Bennington College Writing Seminars.

Schwartz writes: "As far as I can remember, 'The Afterlife' did begin as a dream, just as in the poem. How can anyone remember a dream almost a year old? All I recall is that I was in the afterlife searching for my mother, and my great shock and dismay that she didn't seem at all pleased to see me. I'm not sure whether in the dream I was actually dead or just paying a visit to the dead, but in either case, what a disappointment that my mother greeted me in so perfunctory a way."

FREDERICK SEIDEL was born in St. Louis, Missouri, in 1936. He earned an undergraduate degree at Harvard University in 1957. He is the author of numerous collections of poetry, including *Ooga-Booga* (Farrar, Straus and Giroux, 2006), winner of the *Los Angeles Times* Book Prize; and also from Farrar, Straus and Giroux, *The Cosmos Trilogy* (2003) and *Going Fast* (1998).

BRENDA SHAUGHNESSY was born in Okinawa, Japan, in 1970. Her most recent collection of poetry is *Our Andromeda* (Copper Canyon Press, 2012). She is also the author of *Human Dark with Sugar* (Copper Canyon Press, 2008) and *Interior with Sudden Joy* (Farrar, Straus and Giroux, 2000). She is poetry editor-at-large at *Tin House* magazine and teaches at Rutgers University in Newark, New Jersey. She lives in Brooklyn with her husband and their two children.

Shaughnessy writes: " 'Artless' is about failing to turn painful experience into art and wondering if the art about that failure can produce a kind of new treatment for the hurt it can't erase, perhaps by writing over it, stanza by stanza, making room for other things, and lessening the power of the hurt. Thus the mantra-math of repeating '-less' '-less' '-less.'

"I was wondering what exactly allows such intense pain and such vast hope to coexist in the same small life, sometimes in the same moment. And why is there so little to hold on to through all the wounding and grieving and rejoicing and loving and gratitude? What is the center and what the periphery? What is the meat and what the gristle? If I understand the heart as both our locus and our pump, this doubleness is a cruel trick: having a 'crux' means the rest of what constitutes us is appendage or garbage or baggage. And yet this central self, the heart, is also capable of standing apart, regarding, and performing itself and our emotions, our lives. Performing love.

"This thought crushes me.

"And so what about this possibility of art? If there is no unified self to 'be' fully self and heart at once always, why not embrace a poeticizing of our experience, why not be used by art? Push our lived life through the art and let what is extruded be beautiful?

"Because being used makes us feel empty.

"If the two meanings of 'heart' are 'center' and 'part,' the word 'art' also frames a perplexing doubleness: it is something human-made with materials but also with inner resources; that is, it is made of us. Art *is* life. And yet it is distinct from 'life.' It is life's counterpoint. We make it, and in that making, art is pointedly *not* life. It is *just made of us.*

"The word 'artless' is tricky. The correct if old-fashioned meaning is innocence, free of guile or artifice. It is a word that means purity, but sounds like it means inelegant, clumsy, or unbeautiful: something that fails to be art.

"One would think art could help manage life by transforming it into something beautiful and useful. But regular life has no such costume to slip into, no set to disappear into.

"I'm artless, because real pain is not imaginary. I suffer it purely and without artifice. And yet I dress it up and give it speech and qualities as if it is an imaginary friend. I know my pure, true 'artless' self less and less and less with every stanza I write, trying to make this pain beautiful."

PETER JAY SHIPPY was born in Niagara Falls in 1961 and was raised on his family's apple farm. He was educated at Northwestern University, Emerson College, and the University of Iowa. He is the author of *Thieves' Latin* (University of Iowa Press, 2003), *Alphaville* (BlazeVOX Books, 2006), and *How to Build the Ghost in Your Attic* (Rose Metal Press, 2007). He has received fellowships from the Massachusetts Cultural Council and from the National Endowment for the Arts. He teaches literature and creative writing at Emerson College and lives in Jamaica Plain, Massachusetts, with his wife, Charlotte, and their daughters, Beatrix and Stella.

Of "Our Posthumous Lives," Shippy writes: "As everyone knows, poets have a moral obligation to be 37 percent truthful. This elegy weighs in, faithfully, at 39 percent. It sports a white sheet, but underneath is the honest-to-goodness ghost of my dear friend, sorely missed."

TRACY K. SMITH was born in Falmouth, Massachusetts, in 1972 and was raised in Fairfield, California. She attended Harvard and Columbia Universities and was a Wallace Stegner fellow in poetry at Stanford University. She teaches creative writing at Princeton University. She is the author of three collections of poetry: *Life on Mars* (Graywolf Press, 2011), *Duende* (Graywolf Press, 2007), and *The Body's Question* (Graywolf Press, 2003). *Life on Mars* won the 2012 Pulitzer Prize in poetry.

Smith writes: "In 'Everything That Ever Was,' I was interested in exploring some of the darker implications of elegy. What if there was an afterlife not just for the loved ones we have lost, but also for the events and relationships we are happy now to be rid of? What would it mean if the past continued to live on, aware of us but separated from our realm by the same thing that separates us from our beloved dead? The poem imagines a scenario in which the past tries to make contact with the present in the same ways a ghost or spirit of the deceased might reach out to the living."

BRUCE SNIDER was born in Columbia City, Indiana, in 1971. He is the author of two books, *Paradise, Indiana* (Pleaides Press/Louisiana State University Press, 2012) and *The Year We Studied Women* (University of Wisconsin Press, 2003). He lives in San Francisco and teaches at Stanford University.

Of "The Drag Queen Dies in New Castle," Snider writes: "When I was in my early teens, a classmate's older brother returned home quite ill from studying dance in New York City and died (of what, no one would say). A rumor went around school that he'd come home with a trunk full of women's clothes. I have no idea if this was true, but the strangeness of that rumor and the silence accompanying his death spooked me in ways I couldn't articulate at the time. I suppose that this poem—one of several I've been writing about the lives of gay men in rural America—is my way of filling that silence."

MARK STRAND was born in 1934 in Summerside, Prince Edward Island, Canada. He lives in New York City and teaches at Columbia University.

Of "The Mysterious Arrival of an Unusual Letter," Strand writes:

"Years ago I wanted to write a poem in which my father, though long dead, writes to me from an undisclosed location, admitting that he has been in hiding but is still alive. I could never figure out what he would say in such a letter. As I was writing *Almost Invisible* (Alfred A. Knopf, 2012), I suddenly remembered the poem about my father. I wrote 'The Mysterious Arrival of an Unusual Letter' in one quick sitting."

LARISSA SZPORLUK was born in Ann Arbor, Michigan, in 1967. She is an associate professor of creative writing and English at Bowling Green State University and is the author of five books of poetry. Her most recent book, *Traffic with Macbeth,* was published by Tupelo Press in 2011. She received a Guggenheim Fellowship in 2009 and a National Endowment for the Arts grant in 2003. She is a mother of three.

Of "Sunflower," Szporluk writes: "This poem was written in the spring of 2009 when my newborn, Sebastian, was quite ill. Because I was mostly in the hospital during that time, the poem began in my head and never made it to paper until it was completely done. And it wasn't done until I realized that I wasn't in the poem at all, nor was Sebastian; I had just accessed some kind of dark little mystery play that was taking place somewhere and the poem just knew to end when the sunflower's honesty was being questioned."

DANIEL TOBIN was born in Brooklyn, New York, in 1958. He is the author of six books of poems: *Where the World Is Made* (Middlebury College Press, 1999), *Double Life* (Louisiana State University Press, 2004), *The Narrows* (Four Way Books, 2005), *Second Things* (Four Way Books, 2008), *Belated Heavens* (Four Way Books, 2010), and *The Net* (forthcoming from Four Way Books in 2014). He is also the author of the critical studies *Awake in America: On Irish American Poetry* (University of Notre Dame Press, 2011) and *Passage to the Center: Imagination and the Sacred in the Poetry of Seamus Heaney* (University Press of Kentucky, 1999). He is the editor of *The Book of Irish American Poetry from the Eighteenth Century to the Present* (University of Notre Dame Press, 2007), *Light in Hand, Selected Early Poems of Lola Ridge* (Quale Press, 2007), and *Poet's Work, Poet's Play: Essays on the Practice and the Art* (University of Michigan Press, 2008, with Pimone Triplett). He is currently Interim Dean of the School of the Arts at Emerson College.

Of "The Turnpike," Tobin writes: "One of the first poets whose work I fell in love with was John Donne. For all of his immense imaginative ingenuity and formal mastery there is something shamelessly intense about the poems—they are demanding intellectually and emotionally, physically and metaphysically, and immoderately so. Line after line of a Donne poem coveys the feeling that he is intent on outrunning the proverbial 'dissociation of sensibility' Eliot saw settling into Western culture after him, pedal to the metal across hairpin turns of rhythm, syntax, and conceit.

"Donne's 'A Valediction: Forbidding Mourning,' which 'The Turnpike' purposely echoes, rides on its own extended metaphor, though more as a pending salutation than as a valediction. Among other things the poem updates Donne's physical metaphysics with its own metaphysical physics. Call it transportation as superposition, a doubling and redoubling of reality into parallel possibilities, though the poem refuses to drive wholly away from the palpable. Where does it arrive? Not at Donne's twin compasses come round again, but at a spark of perpetual motion, and below that the universal engine's catalytic stillness, inexhaustible: call it love's pure fuel."

NATASHA TRETHEWEY was born in Gulfport, Mississippi, in 1966. She is the author of *Beyond Katrina: A Meditation on the Mississippi Gulf Coast* (University of Georgia Press, 2010) and three collections of poetry, *Domestic Work* (Graywolf Press, 2000), *Bellocq's Ophelia* (Graywolf Press, 2002), and *Native Guard* (Houghton Mifflin, 2006). *Native Guard* was awarded the Pulitzer Prize. At Emory University she is the Charles Howard Candler Professor of English and Creative Writing. Her new book, *Thrall*, is forthcoming from Houghton Mifflin Harcourt in 2012.

Trethewey writes: "The poem, 'Dr. Samuel Adolphus Cartwright on Dissecting the White Negro, 1851,' is primarily about language, and it arises from a consideration of the darker legacy of Enlightenment thinking—the taxonomy and codification of ideas of race and difference (and white supremacy). The anatomist's lecture in the poem echoes my own sense of having been not only an object of curiosity (*What are you?* the constant question posed by strangers) but also a person subjected to being parsed in the American lexicon, by the nomenclature of miscegenation."

SUSAN WHEELER was born in Pittsburgh, Pennsylvania, in 1955. She grew up mostly in Minnesota and has lived in or near New York since 1985. She is on the faculty of Princeton University, where she directs the creative writing program. She has received awards from the American Academy of Arts and Letters and the Guggenheim Foundation. Her poetry collections include *Bag 'o' Diamonds* (University of Georgia Press, 1993), *Smokes* (Four Way Books, 1998), *Source Codes* (Salt Publishing, 2001), *Ledger* (University of Iowa Press, 2005), *Assorted Poems* (Farrar, Straus and Giroux, 2009), and *Meme* (University of Iowa Press, 2012). She is also the author of a novel, *Record Palace* (Graywolf Press, 2005).

Of "The Split," Wheeler writes: "Each major loss resonates, like overtones on a string, with deaths a person has known."

FRANZ WRIGHT notes that he "was born in Vienna in the spring of 1953. My father had a Fulbright, and he and my mother—newlywed high-school sweethearts from Martins Ferry, Ohio—couldn't have been more than twenty-two or twenty-three years old, a fact I find staggering. I suppose people born in the late twenties and thirties of the twentieth century became full-blown adults by the time they reached puberty, in keeping with historical events.

"I live in Waltham, Massachusetts—my wife and I have lived here for the past eleven or twelve years—and cannot say I have an occupation, although I led the graduate poetry workshop at the University of Arkansas, in Fayetteville, spring 2004, and served as poet-in-residence at Brandeis University, here in Waltham, for a time, and was associated with the Center for Grieving Children & Teenagers, in Arlington, for a number of years. I have been publishing with Knopf since 2001." Wright's *Walking to Martha's Vineyard* won the Pulitzer Prize in 2004. *Kindertotenwald,* a book of prose poems, appeared in September 2011. Two new collections are in the works.

Of "The Lesson," Wright notes: "All I can say about my prose poem is that it is based on a true story, the terribly painful life of an eighth-grade friend of mine in Walnut Creek, California. She was a tough girl and she made it, God knows how. She told me about this event only years later, and I have not retained all the details. We're still friends."

DAVID YEZZI was born in Albany, New York, in 1966. His books of poems are *The Hidden Model* (TriQuarterly Books, 2003) and *Azores* (Swallow Press, 2008). He is the editor of *The Swallow Anthology of New American Poets* (2009). A former director of the Unterberg Poetry Center of the 92nd Street Y, he is executive editor of *The New Criterion,* and he teaches in the low-residency MFA program at Western State College of Colorado. He lives in New York City with his wife, Sarah, and their three children.

Of "Minding Rites," Yezzi writes: "The rabbi in the poem is based on my friend Phil Miller, with whom I used to work. On Fridays, a few of us would gather in Phil's office to read and discuss passages from the Bible, always an enlivening hour given his perception and warmth. Phil is a model family man, who dotes on his wife and children. The anecdote about the flowers is basically true, though the breakup at the end is more a weighing of the possibility. The poem, like an anxious talisman, keeps me mindful of my failings and is a reminder that poems are not flowers—which is to say, I need to make a stop on my way home."

DEAN YOUNG was born in Columbia, Pennsylvania, in 1955. He teaches at the University of Texas, Austin, where he holds the William Livingston Chair of Poetry. His most recent book is *Fall Higher,* published by Copper Canyon Press in 2011. His selected poems, *Bender,* will be published in 2012 by Copper Canyon Press.

Of "Restoration Ode," Young writes: "A lot of poets sometimes feel their poems have clairvoyant moments and can predict the course of events. No matter what Auden says, I believe poems can make things happen. In 'Restoration Ode' I set out to make something happen through a kind of spell. But as with all hocus-pocus, what happens doesn't usually happen in the way you'd think."

KEVIN YOUNG was born in Lincoln, Nebraska, in 1970. His books of poetry include *Most Way Home* (William Morrow, 1995), *Jelly Roll: A Blues* (Alfred A. Knopf, 2003), *For the Confederate Dead* (which won the 2007 Quill Award for poetry), and *Dear Darkness* (Alfred A. Knopf, 2008), which won a 2009 Southern Independent Booksellers Alliance Award in poetry. His most recent book is *Ardency: A Chronicle of the Amistad Rebels* (Alfred A. Knopf, 2011). Young has edited *The Art of Losing: Poems of Grief and Healing,* an anthology of contemporary elegies (Bloomsbury USA, 2010), as well as the collections *Jazz Poems* (2006) and *Blues Poems* (2003) from Everyman's Library, a selected edition of John Berryman's poems for the Library of America's American Poets Project, and *Giant Steps: The New Generation of African American Writers* (HarperCollins, 2000). His book *The Grey Album: On the Blackness of Blackness* won the 2010 Graywolf Nonfiction Prize. A recipient of a Guggenheim Fellowship, he is the Atticus Haygood Professor of Creative Writing and English and is curator of literary collections and the Raymond Danowski Poetry Library at Emory University in Atlanta. He was guest editor of *The Best American Poetry 2011.*

MAGAZINES WHERE THE POEMS
WERE FIRST PUBLISHED

The American Poetry Review, eds. Stephen Berg, David Bonanno, and Elizabeth Scanlon. 1700 Sansom Street, Suite 800, Philadelphia, PA 19103.

The Antioch Review, poetry ed. Judith Hall. PO Box 148, Yellow Springs, OH 45387.

Barrow Street, eds. Lorna Knowles Blake, Patricia Carlin, Peter Covino, Melissa Hotchkiss, and Lois Hirshkowitz (1998–2006). PO Box 1831, New York, NY 10156.

Beloit Poetry Journal, eds. John Rosenwald and Lee Sharkey. PO Box 151, Farmington, ME 04938.

Boston Review, poetry eds. Timothy Donnelly and Benjamin Paloff. 35 Medford Street, Suite 302, Somerville, MA 02143.

The Cincinnati Review, poetry ed. Don Bogen. PO Box 210069, Cincinnati, OH 45221-0069.

Colorado Review, poetry eds. Donald Revell, Sasha Steensen, and Matthew Cooperman. 9105 Campus Delivery, Department of English, Colorado State University, Fort Collins, CO 80523-9105.

The Common, poetry ed. John Hennessy. Frost Library, Amherst College, Amherst, MA 01002.

Conduit, ed. William Waltz. 510 Eighth Avenue NE, Minneapolis, MN 55413.

Five Points, eds. David Bottoms and Megan Sexton. PO Box 3999, Atlanta, GA 30302-3999.

The Gettysburg Review, ed. Peter Stitt. Gettysburg College, Gettysburg, PA 17325-1491.

Granta, ed. John Freeman. 12 Addison Avenue, London W11 4QR England.

Green Mountains Review, poetry ed. Elizabeth Powell. 337 College Hill, Johnson, VT 05656.

Gulf Coast, poetry eds. Joshua Gottlieb-Miller, Janine Joseph, and Karyna McGlynn. Department of English, University of Houston, Houston, TX 77204-3013.

Harvard Review, poetry ed. Major Jackson. Lamont Library, Harvard University, Cambridge, MA 02138.

The Hudson Review, ed. Paula Deitz. 684 Park Avenue, New York, NY 10021.

The Kenyon Review, poetry ed. David Baker. www.kenyonreview.org.

Lambda Literary Review, poetry eds. David Groff and Jameson Fitzpatrick. www.lambdaliterary.org

The Literary Review, poetry eds. Renée Ashley and David Daniel. Fairleigh Dickinson University, 285 Madison Avenue, Madison, NJ 07940.

Mead: The Magazine of Literature and Libations, editor-in-chief Laura McCullough. www.meadmagazine.org

Memorious, editor-in-chief Rebecca Morgan Frank. www.memorious. org.

The Nation, poetry ed. Jordan Davis. 33 Irving Place, New York, NY 10003-2307.

New American Writing, eds. Maxine Chernoff and Paul Hoover. 369 Molino Avenue, Mill Valley, CA 94941.

New England Review, poetry ed. C. Dale Young. Middlebury College, Middlebury, VT 05753.

New Ohio Review, ed. Jill Allyn Rosser. English Department, 360 Ellis Hall, Ohio University, Athens, OH 45701.

The New Yorker, poetry ed. Paul Muldoon. 4 Times Square, New York, NY 10036.

Ploughshares, poetry ed. John Skoyles. Emerson College, 120 Boylston Street, Boston, MA 02116-4624.

Poetry, ed. Christian Wiman. 444 North Michigan Avenue, Suite 1850, Chicago, IL 60611-4034.

Poetry Daily, coeditors Don Selby and Diane Boller. www.poems.com.

Prairie Schooner, ed. Hilda Raz. 201 Andrews Hall, PO Box 880334, Lincoln, NE 68588-0334.

River Styx, ed. Richard Newman. 3547 Olive Street, Suite 107, St. Louis, MO 63103.

Salmagundi, eds. Robert Boyers and Peg Boyers. Skidmore College, 815 North Broadway, Saratoga Springs, NY 12866.

Seneca Review, ed. David Weiss. Hobart and William Smith Colleges, English Department, 101 Demarest Hall, Geneva, NY 14456.

The Southern Review, poetry ed. Jessica Faust. 3990 West Lakeshore Drive, Louisiana State University, Baton Rouge, LA 70808.

Southwest Review, ed. Willard Spiegelman. PO Box 750374, Dallas, TX 75275-0374.

Subtropics, poetry ed. Sidney Wade. PO Box 112075, 4008 Turlington Hall, University of Florida, Gainesville, FL 32611-2075.

The Threepenny Review, ed. Wendy Lesser. PO Box 9131, Berkeley, CA 94709.

Tin House, poetry ed. Matthew Dickman. PO Box 10500, Portland, OR 97210.

Umbrella, ed. Kate Bernadette Benedict. www.umbrellajournal.com.

Witness, poetry ed. Joshua Kryah. Black Mountain Institute, University of Nevada, Box 455085, Las Vegas, NV 89154-5085.

Zoland Poetry, ed. Roland Pease. www.zolandpoetry.com.

ACKNOWLEDGMENTS

The series editor thanks Mark Bibbins for his invaluable assistance. Warm thanks go also to Stacey Harwood and Stephanie Paterik; to Glen Hartley and Lynn Chu of Writers' Representatives; and to my editor, Alexis Gargagliano, and her colleagues at Scribner, including Daniel Cuddy, Erich Hobbing, Kelsey Smith, and David Stanford Burr.

Grateful acknowledgment is made of the magazines in which these poems first appeared and the magazine editors who selected them. A sincere attempt has been made to locate all copyright holders. Unless otherwise noted, copyright to the poems is held by the individual poets.

Sherman Alexie: "Terminal Nostalgia" appeared in *Green Mountains Review*. Reprinted by permission of the poet.

Karen Leona Anderson: "Receipt: Midway Entertainment Presents" appeared in *Seneca Review*. Reprinted by permission of the poet.

Rae Armantrout: "Accounts" appeared in *Poetry*. Reprinted by permission of the poet.

Julianna Baggott: "For Furious Nursing Baby" appeared in *The Cincinnati Review*. Reprinted by permission of the poet.

David Baker: "Outside" appeared in *The Southern Review*. Reprinted by permission of the poet.

Rick Barot: "Child Holding Potato" appeared in *Memorious*. Reprinted by permission of the poet.

Reginald Dwayne Betts: "At the End of Life, a Secret" appeared in *New England Review*. Reprinted by permission of the poet.

Frank Bidart: "Of His Bones Are Coral Made" appeared in *Salmagundi*. Reprinted by permission of the poet.

Bruce Bond: "Pill" appeared in *Colorado Review*. Reprinted by permission of the poet.

Stephanie Brown: "Notre Dame" appeared in *The American Poetry Review*. Reprinted by permission of the poet.

Anne Carson: "Sonnet of Exemplary Sentences" appeared in *The Nation*. Reprinted by permission of the poet.

Jennifer Chang: "Dorothy Wordsworth" appeared in *The Nation*. Reprinted by permission of the poet.

Joseph Chapman: "Sparrow" appeared in *The Cincinnati Review.* Reprinted by permission of the poet.

Heather Christle: "BASIC" from *What Is Amazing.* © 2012 by Heather Christle. Reprinted by permission of Wesleyan University Press. Also appeared in *The New Yorker.*

Henri Cole: "Broom" from *Touch.* © 2011 by Henri Cole. Reprinted by permission of Farrar, Straus and Giroux. Also appeared in *The Threepenny Review.*

Billy Collins: "Delivery" appeared in *Subtropics.* Reprinted by permission of the poet.

Peter Cooley: "More Than Twice, More Than I Can Count" appeared in *Harvard Review.* Reprinted by permission of the poet.

Eduardo C. Corral: "To the Angelbeast" from *Slow Lightning.* © 2011 by Eduardo C. Corral. Reprinted by permission of Yale University Press. Also appeared in *Poetry.*

Erica Dawson: "Back Matter" appeared in *Barrow Street.* Reprinted by permission of the poet.

Stephen Dunn: "The Imagined" from *Here and Now.* © 2011 by Stephen Dunn. Reprinted by permission of W. W. Norton & Co. Also appeared in *The New Yorker.*

Elaine Equi: "A Story Begins" appeared in *New American Writing.* Reprinted by permission of the poet.

Robert Gibb: "Spirit in the Dark" from *Sheet Music.* © 2012 by Robert Gibb. Reprinted with the permission of The Permissions Company, Inc., on behalf of Autumn House Press. Also appeared in *Prairie Schooner.*

Kathleen Graber: "Self-Portrait with No Internal Navigation" appeared in *Mead.* Reprinted by permission of the poet.

Amy Glynn Greacen: "*Helianthus annuus* (Sunflower)" appeared in *New England Review.* Reprinted by permission of the poet.

James Allen Hall: "One Train's Survival Depends on the Other Derailed" appeared in *New England Review.* Reprinted by permission of the poet.

Terrance Hayes: "The Rose Has Teeth" appeared in *Tin House.* Reprinted by permission of the poet.

Steven Heighton: "Collision" from *Patient Frame.* © 2010 by Steven Heighton. Reprinted by permission of House of Anansi Press. Also appeared in *The Literary Review.*

Brenda Hillman: "Moaning Action at the Gas Pump" appeared in *Gulf Coast.* Reprinted by permission of the poet.

Jane Hirshfield: "In a Kitchen Where Mushrooms Were Washed" appeared in *Ploughshares*. Reprinted by permission of the poet.

Richard Howard: "A Proposed Curriculum Change" appeared in *The Antioch Review*. Reprinted by permission of the poet.

Marie Howe: "Magdalene—The Seven Devils" appeared in *The American Poetry Review*. Reprinted by permission of the poet.

Amorak Huey: "Memphis" appeared in *The Southern Review*. Reprinted by permission of the poet.

Jenny Johnson: "Aria" appeared in *Beloit Poetry Journal*. Reprinted by permission of the poet.

Lawrence Joseph: "So Where Are We?" appeared in *Granta*. Reprinted by permission of the poet.

Fady Joudah: "Tenor" appeared in *Beloit Poetry Journal* and *Poetry Daily*. Reprinted by permission of the poet.

Joy Katz: "Death Is Something Entirely Else" appeared in *The Cincinnati Review*. Reprinted by permission of the poet.

James Kimbrell: "How to Tie a Knot" appeared in *The Cincinnati Review*. Reprinted by permission of the poet.

Noelle Kocot: "Poem" appeared in *New American Writing*. Reprinted by permission of the poet.

Maxine Kumin: "Either Or" appeared in *Ploughshares*. Reprinted by permission of the poet.

Sarah Lindsay: "Hollow Boom Soft Chime: The Thai Elephant Orchestra" appeared in *Poetry*. Reprinted by permission of the poet.

Amit Majmudar: "The Autobiography of Khwaja Mustasim" appeared in *The New Yorker*. Reprinted by permission of the poet.

David Mason: "Mrs. Mason and the Poets" appeared in *The Hudson Review* and *Umbrella*. Reprinted by permission of the poet.

Kerrin McCadden: "Becca" appeared in *The American Poetry Review*. Reprinted by permission of the poet.

Honor Moore: "Song" appeared in *The Common*. Reprinted by permission of the poet.

Michael Morse: "Void and Compensation (Facebook)" appeared in *Ploughshares*. Reprinted by permission of the poet.

Carol Muske-Dukes: "Hate Mail" appeared in *Boston Review*. Reprinted by permission of the poet.

Angelo Nikolopoulos: "Daffodil" appeared in *Lambda Literary Review*. Reprinted by permission of the poet.

Mary Oliver: "In Provincetown, and Ohio, and Alabama" from *Swan*.

© 2010 by Mary Oliver. Reprinted by permission of Beacon Press. Also appeared in *Five Points.*

Steve Orlen: "Where Do We Go After We Die" appeared in *New Ohio Review.* Reprinted by permission of the literary estate of Steve Orland.

Alicia Ostriker: "Song" appeared in *Poetry* and *Poetry Daily.* Reprinted by permission of the poet.

Eric Pankey: "Sober Then Drunk Again" appeared in *The Cincinnati Review.* Reprinted by permission of the poet.

Lucia Perillo: "Samara" from *On the Spectrum of Possible Deaths.* © 2012 by Lucia Perillo. Reprinted with the permission of The Permissions Company, Inc., on behalf of Copper Canyon Press. Also appeared in *The American Poetry Review.*

Robert Pinsky: "Improvisation on Yiddish" appeared in *The Threepenny Review.* Reprinted by permission of the poet.

Dean Rader: "Self-Portrait as Dido to Aeneas" from *Works & Days.* © 2010 by Dean Rader. Reprinted by permission of Truman State University Press. Also appeared in *The Cincinnati Review.*

Spencer Reece: "The Road to Emmaus" appeared in *Poetry.* Reprinted by permission of the poet.

Paisley Rekdal: "Wax" from *Animal Eye.* © 2012 by Paisley Rekdal. Reprinted by permission of the University of Pittsburgh Press. Also appeared in *Witness.*

Mary Ruefle: "Middle School" appeared in *Conduit.* Reprinted by permission of the poet.

Don Russ: "Girl with Gerbil" appeared in *The Cincinnati Review.* Reprinted by permission of the poet.

Kay Ryan: "Playacting" appeared in *The Threepenny Review.* Reprinted by permission of the poet.

Mary Jo Salter: "The Gods" appeared in *The Common.* Reprinted by permission of the poet.

Lynne Sharon Schwartz: "The Afterlife" from *See You in the Dark.* © 2012 by Lynne Sharon Schwartz. Reprinted by permission of Northwestern University Press. Also appeared in *River Styx.*

Frederick Seidel: "Rain" appeared in *The New Yorker.* Reprinted by permission of the poet.

Brenda Shaughnessy: "Artless" from *Our Andromeda.* © 2012 by Brenda Shaughnessy. Reprinted with the permission of The Permissions Company, Inc., on behalf of Copper Canyon Press. Also appeared in *The New Yorker.*

Peter Jay Shippy: "Our Posthumous Lives" appeared in *The Literary Review*. Reprinted by permission of the poet.

Tracy K. Smith: "Everything That Ever Was" from *Life on Mars*. © 2011 by Tracy K. Smith. Reprinted with the permission of The Permissions Company, Inc., on behalf of Graywolf Press. Also appeared in *Zoland Poetry*.

Bruce Snider: "The Drag Queen Dies in New Castle" appeared in *The Gettysburg Review*. Reprinted by permission of the poet.

Mark Strand: "The Mysterious Arrival of an Unusual Letter" from *Almost Invisible*. © 2012 by Mark Strand. Reprinted by permission of Alfred A. Knopf, a division of Random House, Inc. Also appeared in *Poetry*.

Larissa Szporluk: "Sunflower" from *Traffic with Macbeth*. © 2011 by Larissa Szporluk. Reprinted by permission of Tupelo Press. Also appeared in *Ploughshares*.

Daniel Tobin: "The Turnpike" appeared in *Southwest Review*. Reprinted by permission of the poet.

Natasha Trethewey: "Dr. Samuel Adolphus Cartwright on Dissecting the White Negro, 1851" from *Thrall*. © 2012 by Natasha Trethewey. Reprinted by permission of Houghton Mifflin Harcourt. Also appeared in *New England Review*.

Susan Wheeler: From "The Split" from *Meme*. © 2012 by Susan Wheeler. Reprinted by permission of the University of Iowa Press. Also appeared in *The New Yorker*.

Franz Wright: "The Lesson" from *Kindertotenwald*. © 2011 by Franz Wright. Reprinted by permission of Alfred A. Knopf, a division of Random House, Inc. Also appeared in *The Kenyon Review*.

David Yezzi: "Minding Rites" appeared in *New Ohio Review*. Reprinted by permission of the poet.

Dean Young: "Restoration Ode" appeared in *The Gettysburg Review* and *Poetry Daily*. Reprinted by permission of the poet.

Kevin Young: "Expecting" appeared in *The New Yorker*. Reprinted by permission of the poet.